Patricia Simpson • Louise Pothier

Patricia Simpson, C.N.D

NOTRE-DAME-DE-BON-SECOURS

A Chapel and its Neighbourhood

CHAPELLE
NOTRE-DAME-DE-BON-SECOURS
MUSÉE
MARGUERITE-BOURGEOYS

FIDES

Project director
Danielle Dubois

Authors
Patricia Simpson
Louise Pothier

Co-ordinator
Claire Dumesnil

Research assistants
Rachel Gaudreau
Madeleine Huet
Eileen McGurk

Contributors
Jacques Des Rochers
Claude Joyal
Monique Lanthier
Pierre-Jacques Ratio
Rémi Tougas
François Véronneau

Cover illustration: *La Chapelle Notre-Dame-de-Bonsecours vue du port de Montréal*, about 1885. Water-colour by Napoléon Bourassa. Photograph: Patrick Altman. Musée du Québec, n° 43.55.217

Graphic Design: Folio infographie

Canadian Cataloguing in Publication data

Patricia Simpson and Louise Pothier

    Notre-Dame-de-Bon-Secours: a Chapel and its Neighbourhood
    Includes bibliographical references.

    ISBN 2-7621-2224-4

1. Notre-Dame-de-Bon-Secours Chapel (Montreal, Quebec) History.
2. Church architecture - Quebec (Province) - Montréal.
3. Chapels - Quebec (Province) - Montreal - History.
4. Vieux-Montréal (Montreal, Quebec) - History.

NA5247.M65S5513 2001   726'.4'0971428   C2001940500-6

Legal deposit: second quarter 2001
National Library of Québec

The publisher gratefully acknowledges the support of the Canada Council for the Arts and of the Société de développment des entreprises culturelles (Québec). The publisher also acknowledges the support of the Government of Canada through the Book Publishing Industry Development Program.

PRINTED IN CANADA

CONTENTS

ACKNOWLEDGEMENTS

A NUMBER OF PEOPLE read and offered comments on preliminary versions of this work. The Marguerite Bourgeoys Museum gratefully acknowledges the contributions of Anne-Marie Balac, Roger Lachapelle, Gilles Lauzon, Paul-André Linteau, Rolland Litalien, Eileen McGurk, Joyce Roberts, Léon Robichaud, Brian Ross, Roland Tremblay and Jacques Viger. The museum is also grateful to Francis Back, Claude Paulette, Notre-Dame Basilica, Pointe-à-Callière, Montréal Museum of Archaeology and History and to the Service du développement économique et urbain de la Ville de Montréal for the loan of photographs and copies of original works. The Museum also thanks the Ville de Montréal, la Société de Développement de Montréal and the Direction de Montréal du ministère de la Culture et des Communications du Québec for their support of the project.

This publication was made possible through a grant received as part of the Entente sur le développement culturel de Montréal undertaken between le ministère de la Culture et des Communications du Québec and the Ville de Montréal.

INTRODUCTION

W HEN VILLE-MARIE was still in its first perilous years of existence, Marguerite Bourgeoys decided to build a chapel of pilgrimage dedicated to the Blessed Virgin Mary on the shores of the Saint Lawrence. The realization of that intention was fraught with difficulties and required as much patience and tenacity as it did stone and mortar. Yet the building that rose a few hundred paces from the little settlement became Montreal's first stone church and Marguerite Bourgeoys' desire that its site be consecrated to Mary "in perpetuity" has prevailed over the centuries. The site of Notre-Dame-de-Bon-Secours Chapel is the oldest site in Montreal to have maintained its original vocation.

From its beginnings, the chapel was visited daily by Montrealers and, before long, they began to settle close by. The *faubourg* Bonsecours was born. From then on, the development of the chapel and of the *quartier* went hand in hand, so that to study the history of the chapel is also to study the development of Montreal of which it is, in a sense, a microcosm. Consumed by fire, then rebuilt, repeatedly threatened with demolition in the name of urban development, the chapel has displayed an extaordinary power to survive: a witness to the Marian devotion that inspired the naming of Ville-Marie and that even after three and one-half centuries finds an echo in such late twentieth-century phenomena as Place Ville-Marie and the Ville-Marie Expressway.

This is the history of a building, its development and transformation, but it is also a history of the context in which these things happened, the history of a district and of the city that grew with and around the chapel. At the centre of the history of Notre-Dame-de-Bon-Secours Chapel are the people of Montreal, the men, women and children who lived in the *quartier*, the neighbourhood, of which the chapel was the heart and soul. It has been a district of cultural diversity, a place where old traditions lived on but where new arrivals found a haven. The capacity of the chapel to assume powerful symbolic importance in the minds of Montrealers, new and old, has been an important factor in its survival.

In the nineteenth century, the chapel became a popular subject for painters and photographers and some artists, like William Berczy and James Duncan, even tried to imagine the chapel in the days of Ville-Marie. Today's rediscovery of the history of the chapel in word and image is the result, in great part, of recent discoveries — most of them accidental or unexpected — made during the renovation of the chapel and the attached school. It is now more than a century since a history of the chapel was published. The new discoveries created a particularly opportune moment to bring the story of the chapel up to date and to present historic information not previously available. This new account also comes at a time when the religious heritage of Quebec is at last awakening interest and concern after decades of neglect and destruction. The story of Notre-Dame-de-Bon-Secours Chapel, one of the most ancient and important parts of this heritage, must surely help explain and sustain efforts of preservation. For the many people today who are searching for something beyond material and commercial values, the idea of a pilgrimage in time to the site of Notre-Dame-de-Bon-Secours has its own attraction. To set out, turn the page and see.

NOTE ON NAMES
AND TRANSLATION

The complex linguistic history of Montreal has been reflected in the names of its streets. Some of these originally had French names that were anglicized in the nineteenth century and have, more recently, returned to a French form. In this book, streets that still exist are given the names which are presently found on the street signs of Montreal. Streets which existed during the French regime but have since disappeared are referred to by their French names. The names used for religious communities and institutions are those most familiar to English-speaking Montrealers.

Where alternate spellings of personal names exist, the version chosen is that of *The Dictionary of Canadian Biography*.

Unless otherwise specified, translations of books, articles and documents written in French are ours.

CHAPTER I

IN SEARCH
OF A NEW WORLD

Long, long ago, many generations before the arrival of Europeans on the shores of America, something remarkable happened in the Montreal area. The memory and exact circumstances of this momentous event are lost in the darkness of time, for it must have happened some six thousand years ago, or perhaps even earlier, in the Palaeoindian era eight or nine thousand years ago. It was the first discovery of the Montreal area by human groups of which little is yet known, people who found the rich and hospitable environment so pleasant that they claimed it as a place of refuge.

HUMAN FACES IN A CHANGING LANDSCAPE

Anthropologists and archaeologists are just beginning to study and understand the "colonization" of the Montreal area by *homo sapiens*. Their knowledge increases from year to year as new and certain evidence is added to the record of prehistory. To reconstruct and describe the cultural past of societies that left no written records, investigators must add considerable insight and a good dose of humility and patience to their intellectual baggage. Obviously, the sciences of the past are still young in Quebec and the discoveries that will bring us closer to these peoples of long ago have yet to be made. This does not prevent us from taking advantage of the resources and information already at our disposal.

The raw materials available to feed these fascinating studies can be summed up in two words: places and traces. We already have a good idea of the former in the case of the Old Montreal area, and we

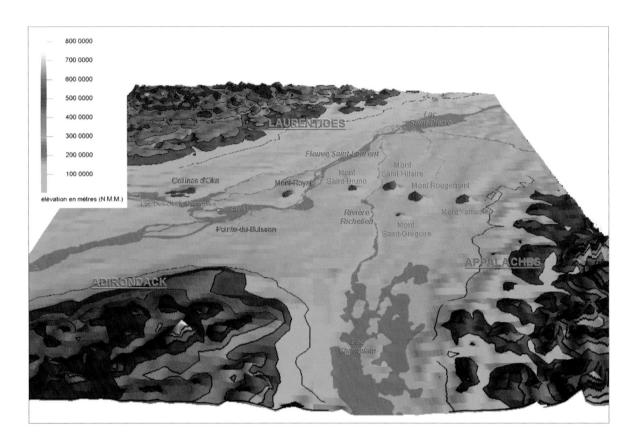

The following labels appear on the illustration:

800 0000
700 0000
600 0000
500 0000
400 0000
300 0000
200 0000
100 0000

élévation en mètres (N.M.M.)

LAURENTIDES

Lac Saint-Pierre

Fleuve Saint-Laurent

Collines d'Oka

Mont-Royal

Mont Saint-Bruno

Mont Saint-Hilaire

Mont Rougemont

Lac Des-Deux Montagnes

Lac Saint-Louis

Rivière Richelieu

Mont Yamaska

Pointe-du-Buisson

Mont Saint-Grégoire

APPALACHES

ADIRONDACK

Lac Champlain

A VAST PLAIN SCATTERED WITH HILLS and buttressed by mountain chains. Such was the territory available for settlement once the ice cap melted and the salt waters and lakes of the Laurentian valley gradually receded between 10,500 and 6000 B.C. The Montreal lowlands drained by the Saint Lawrence River have been accessible to human habitation for the last six to eight thousand years.

Illustration: Pascal Dumont; Marguerite Bourgeoys Museum

are collecting some good indications of the latter. It is to these, then, that we will direct our attention.

Let us return, then, to that hypothetical but likely "founding day" when a group of human beings, coming, probably, from the regions south or west of the Montreal plain, first laid eyes on the Montreal landscape. If the event in question took place between six and eight thousand years ago, as is likely given the favourable natural environment at that time, this is what these newcomers would probably have seen: on the island of Montreal, different terraces showed evidence of the long and progressive emergence from the floods following the melting of the great glaciers; a tissue of vegetation covered the layers of clay and till — a sandy, rocky soil deposited by the glaciers — and favoured the presence of a rich ecosystem.

Thanks to the observations of the palynologists, specialists in the study of ancient pollens, we can reconstitute the surface vegetation of very distant eras, something that also helps us to assess the climate of the time. In about 4000 B.C., the Montreal region was dominated by the sugar maple, as it still is today. The vegetation already carried the seed characteristic of the great maple forests which the French, arriving much later in the upper Saint Lawrence Valley, would reach for superlatives to describe. The maple groves included a large proportion of red oak; white pine dominated the sandy areas; peat bogs were sprinkled with larches. The main difference in surface vegetation between that era and our own is the marked absence of beeches. As for the climate, the presence of maples and, especially, the abundance of pine and oak point to a surprising fact: in the year 4000 B.C. the inhabitants of the region enjoyed more clement summers than is the case today! On a planetary scale, scientists classify this period a climatic optimum.[1]

The territory was vast and the peoples were nomadic. The great river, which the French would later name the Saint Lawrence, and its tributaries were the stage on which the actions of daily life were played out. The waterways allowed access to the different regions, exploration of unknown territory and exchanges with neighbouring or distant groups. Their banks offered refuge and the raw materials for warmth and nourishment. For societies of what is called the Archaic period (4000 to 1000 B.C.), fishing was an important summer activity. Recent excavations at Pointe-du-Buisson and Coteau-du-Lac and in the Richelieu and Ottawa valleys have yielded cultural traces related to groups of the Archaic period. These traces are distinguished chiefly by stone projectile points in a clearly identifiable style: this was the stone age. All around the island of Montreal, there is tangible evidence of the presence of aboriginal peoples; however, archaeologists could not find that there was any human occupation of the island in this period.

1. See *La recherche*, no.321, June 1999.

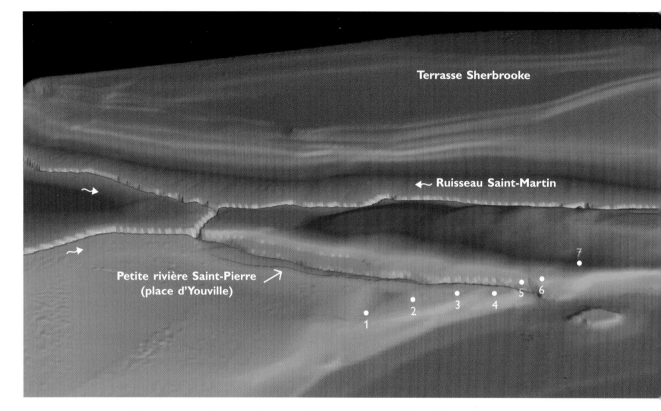

Terrasse Sherbrooke

← Ruisseau Saint-Martin

Petite rivière Saint-Pierre
(place d'Youville)

1 2 3 4 5 6 7

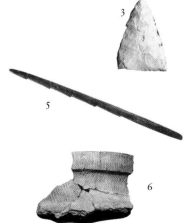

3

5

6

1. JARDINS D'YOUVILLE. The most westerly of the Old Montreal sites; some evidence of **Owascoid** presence, Late Woodland period.

2. RUE DU PORT. Undetermined period of occupation.

3. RUE DE CALLIÈRE. The small **Levanna type projectile point** found on this street could date back to between A.D. 800 and 1600.

4. POINTE À CALLIÈRE. This site has turned up objects from the most recent prehistoric period, the Late Woodland period.

5. PLACE D'YOUVILLE. This **pronged harpoon** made of bone, found in the bed of the former *petite rivière* Saint-Pierre, measures 18.5 cm in length. It could have been used either for fishing or for hunting birds.

6. PLACE ROYALE. To date, the most important prehistoric site in Old Montreal. The lip of an **Iroquoian vase** of Huron influence, represents the last period of occupation.

7. LEMOYNE-LEBER. This site contains the oldest cultural evidence in Old Montreal.

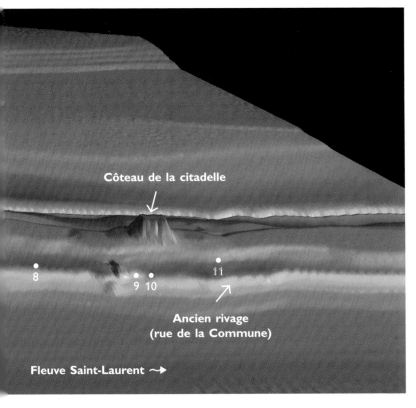

Côteau de la citadelle

Ancien rivage
(rue de la Commune)

Fleuve Saint-Laurent →

Old Montreal in prehistoric times.

The archaeologists who have been digging in Old Montreal since the early 1980s have compiled an inventory of remains that places the time of the first settlements at about 4000 years ago. The prehistoric sites are spread out along the shore and record sporadic periods of occupation by Amerindians. Map based on archaeological data collected by le ministère de la Culture et des Communications du Québec et de la Ville de Montréal.

8. Place Jacques-Cartier. Fragment of a **detachable harpoon tip made of bone**.

9. Notre-Dame-de-Bon-Secours chapel. Site occupied for two thousand years. The **bifaced hornfels knife** shows the possibility of access to local quarries for the production of tools.

10. Accueil Bonneau. The **Onondaga chert scraper** from the Meadowood cultural tradition could date presence on this site to about 1000 B.C.

11. Faubourg Québec. The objects found at the eastern edge of Old Montreal are connected to brief stops made on the site between 500 and 1600 A.D.

Collection of the ministère de la Culture et des Communications du Québec: 9, 10
Collection of the Ville de Montréal: 3 to 8
Photographs 3, 8, 9, 10: Pierre Fauteux, Marguerite Bourgeoys Museum
Photograph 6: Normand Rajotte, Pointe-à-Callière

In Search of a New World ❖ 17

"OLD" MONTREAL IN THE PRIME OF ITS YOUTH

Despite the traces found at many other sites on the Montreal plain, a certain silence reigns over the Archaic period in Old Montreal. For want of evidence, the archives of the soil force us to skip a little more than a thousand years and to begin the human epic later here than elsewhere. This silence probably results from a dearth of archaeological data rather than from a real absence of human population in the area. But we should also remember that, for a long time, the waters of the Saint Lawrence flooded the banks where the buildings of Montreal have been rising for more than three and one-half centuries. Indeed, it seems that, as the waters slowly receded about 4500 years ago, the river surrendered the "terrace" where *rue* Saint-Paul now runs, clearing the way at last for flora and fauna. The river bank, at that time, ran below the present *rue* de la Commune. Opportunist of necessity, human populations were quick to recognize the site, staying there from time to time, depending on the season and on their fishing and hunting expeditions.

The earliest of such locations uncovered in Old Montreal is known as the LeMoyne-LeBer site found at the intersection of Saint-Paul and Saint-Sulpice streets. Two projectile points known as "Lamoka", according to a typology established by archaeologists of the American North-East, were discovered there, permitting the traces of the human occupation of Old Montreal to be dated between 2500 and 1900 B.C. (Post-Laurentian Archaic period). Farther east, two other sites have yielded vestiges two or three thousand years old: under Notre-Dame-de-Bon-Secours Chapel and, a few metres further east, on the Accueil Bonneau site.

There are a total of about ten sites along the edge of the Saint Lawrence frequented several times over during the prehistoric period. Most of the sites are associated with temporary encampments set up, no doubt, by groups of nomads. As yet, there is no archaeological evidence of the presence of semi-sedentary horticultural groups in Old Montreal. The only site yet discovered to have yielded such traces in Montreal is the Dawson site, named for its discoverer, the geologist

"LAMOKA" POINT

Collection of the Ville de Montréal
Photograph: Pierre Fauteaux;
Marguerite Bourgeoys Museum

William Dawson (1820-1899). In this location, situated at the level of Sherbrooke Street not far from McGill University, Dawson discovered, in 1859, the remains of longhouses and burial places, as well as other evidence of an Iroquoian village set up there between about A.D. 1400 and A.D. 1600. Some authors at first believed that this was the Iroquoian village of Hochelaga visited and described by Jacques Cartier in 1535. However, this theory was called into question by ethnohistoric and archaeological analyses carried out in the second half of the twentieth century.[2]

CHRONOLOGY OF THE PREHISTORY OF SOUTHERN QUEBEC

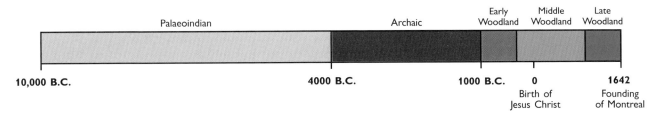

A COVETED TERRACE FOR 3000 YEARS
The historic area of Old Montreal has been the object of archaeological investigation since the early 1980s. It is, in fact, the area in which the greatest concentration of prehistoric sites on the island of Montreal is to be found. In 1997, an ancient natural terrace located in the eastern part of Old Montreal began to yield up fragments of its past under the archaeologist's trowel and eye. This terrace is situated on the very spot where Notre-Dame-de-Bon-Secours Chapel now stands. By its presence, the chapel has helped to preserve the cultural evidence buried in its cellar against the elements and against urbanization.

2. J.F. PENDERGAST and B.G. TRIGGER, *Cartier's Hochelaga and the Dawson Site*, McGill-Queen's University Press, 1972.

In its natural state, the site formed a raised shelf of land stretching toward the bank, a real lookout with a splendid view of the river. The area was covered with a grove of trees, as is suggested by the presence of the *Cenococcum* type mushroom which lives in symbiosis with tree roots and whose spores have been observed in great numbers in the soil samples that archaeologists have collected on the site. Perhaps on a lower level of the embankment, there would also have been wetland vegetation such as bullrushes, macrofossils of which have been identified among the soil samples.

Facing away from the river, the view was completely different. A few paces from the Bonsecours site, one faced an imposing mound which overhung the ridge of Old Montreal. This strange oblong hill, which disappeared from the landscape in about 1820 when it was leveled to permit the eastern extension of *rue* Notre-Dame, was about twenty metres high, judging by old illustrations of Montreal. Its regular shape — the mound resembled a truncated pyramid — and its considerable height at a totally unexpected site make this elevation an object of curiosity. One cannot fail to see in it a disturbing resemblance to the funeral mounds erected by certain Amerindian societies that had made these hillocks a sacred element of their culture from the Mississippi valley to the Upper Saint Lawrence. But what role was played by Mother Nature and what by human hands in this solitary "monument" certainly present long before the arrival of the French on the island of Montreal? Given that the mound has disappeared beyond recovery, we shall perhaps never know the answer. Its precise function in prehistoric societies remains uncertain: a lookout, without doubt; a holy and symbolic place, perhaps; but certainly, a place of some importance to aboriginal groups. Shortly after the founding of Ville-Marie, the French, too, soon found a purpose for the spot because of its commanding height and this, despite its distance from the settlement. A mill was constructed there in 1658, then a small fort equipped with canon platforms in 1693. The mound then became known as the "*coteau de la citadelle*" (Citadel Hill). Is there any deeper connection between this mound and the traces of prehistoric occupation found below it? The only thing of which we are sure is that the hillock must have provided protection against the north-west winds while its summit could have served as an observatory. The vestiges discovered on the archaeological sites of Notre-Dame-de-Bon-Secours Chapel and of the Accueil Bonneau are rich enough to support the assertion that the terrace at the foot of the hill was a place frequented intermittently for three thousand years.

Archaeologists have been able to document four different occupations of the area. As is usual in the study of history, the earliest episode turns out to be the most obscure, a reflection, perhaps, of a very limited presence. The only identifiable cultural object is a small stone scraper of the Meadowood period (between 1000 and 400 B.C.) found at the Accueil Bonneau site. The object is made of Onondaga chert, a raw material that comes from the Niagara escarpment. Once handles were added, scrapers were used to remove the fat from supple materials like skins to make clothing and blankets. Close by, though not necessarily from the same period, archaeologists found a weight for a fishing net or line, abandoned, surprisingly, in the hollow of a firepit. Twenty picket holes discovered here could have contained wooden supports for hanging skins and drying meat or fish.

It is surprising that, apart from several rare stone tools clearly identified with the Meadowood culture, no pottery associated with that cultural tradition has yet been found on the island of Montreal. Indeed, the Meadowood groups were the first to adopt or, perhaps, to introduce the use of ceramic in the American North-East. The use of pottery was then maintained and spread throughout this part of the continent. But it seems that very few of the groups clearly identified with this cultural network frequented the Montreal area, which could explain the small number of traces of their passage.

Generations pass leaving few traces; then the Bonsecours site re-appears on the "map". This time, pottery turns up. Stylistic analysis of the thirty-three shards of a single vase discovered around an ancient firepit confirms the period during which the users made their

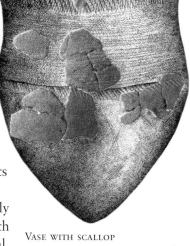

VASE WITH SCALLOP SHELL DECORATION reconstructed from fragments found near the remains of a firepit on the site of Bon-Secours Chapel. The groups that used this decorative technique visited the Bonsecours terrace between 400 B.C. and A.D. 500.

Photograph: Pierre Fauteux; Drawing: Sophie Limoges; Marguerite Bourgeoys Museum

Collection of the ministère de la Culture et des Communications du Québec

stopover on the terrace. Dating from between 400 B.C. and A.D. 500 (Early Middle Woodland period), this fragmentary vase would seem to be one of the most ancient discovered in Old Montreal. Most likely, the higher ground on the edge of the embankment leading to the river was used in ancient times as a rest area where tents were pitched. Not far from there, the presence of another more recent vase used between A.D. 500 and A.D. 1000 (Late Middle Woodland period) confirms that this place was occupied well before the arrival of Europeans.

About ten strides north, toward the hill (the present *rue* Saint-Paul), a more surprising discovery lay in store. Archaeological excavation has raised from the primitive soil traces of an encampment, the only remains of prehistoric habitation yet discovered in Old Montreal. The habitation takes the form of a line of stones marking out a space within which evidence of domestic activities was found. These activities included the digging of a firepit, the fashioning of stone tools resulting in a multitude of fragments, and, possibly, the drying of meat or other foodstuffs, evidence for which is found in the

HYPOTHETICAL RECONSTRUCTION OF A SCENE based on the remains of an encampment found on the Bonsecours site. Without objects that can be dated, however, we know neither the time nor the duration of the stay, nor do we know the ethnic identity of the visitors or the reason for their visit (fishing season? trade?). The remains of the campsite contained materials native to regions outside Montreal, notably a copper nugget (Lake Superior).

Legend:
1. hearth stones?
2. post holes
3. traces of a firepit
4. chips of stone from sharpening tools

Illustration: Francis Back, Marguerite Bourgeoys Museum

holes for pickets used as supports. The line of stones may have served as a weight to hold down the skins covering the wooden framework of a shelter. It is equally possible that these were firepit stones scattered sometime after the occupants left.

This vestige of human habitation has yielded up signs which suggest great cultural energy in its inhabitants. Stone tools fashioned out of materials from distant regions indicate a widespread circle of influence or of political and economic alliances. Among the regions from which "exotic" materials were imported are lower Hudson Bay, Labrador, the Lake Champlain region, the Hudson River Valley in New York State and the Quebec region. Projectile points, knives, scrapers and drills formed a part of the tool chest of those who lived here. A small fragment of native copper was also dug up from the area of habitation. Native copper is a metal of natural origin, surface veins of which were known and exploited for thousands of years by the aboriginal peoples to make jewelery and various tools such as

INSIDE THE PREHISTORIC DWELLING were found about 300 stone fragments of Normanskill chert. This material comes from the west of Lake Champlain and the Hudson Valley. Thus, the craftsman used raw material obtained either in a trade or on his travels. Throughout the pile of fragments were also found tiny traces of charred bone - beaver bone, it would seem.

Collection of the ministère de la Culture et des Communications du Québec

Photograph: Pierre Fauteux, Marguerite Bourgeoys Museum

THE ABUNDANCE OF HORNFELS TOOLS at Bonsecours and on other sites in Old Montreal illustrates the accessibility of this raw material. The Monteregian hills of the Montreal plain were the principal source of supply. Recently, in fact, an extraction site was discovered on Mount Royal.

Collection of the ministère de la Culture et des Communications du Québec

Photograph: Pierre Fauteux, Ville de Montréal

needles, awls, hooks, axes and projectile points. The copper found at Bonsecours probably came from the Lake Superior region of Ontario.

The cultural identity of the inhabitants of this encampment remains a complete mystery. None of the objects discovered in the habitation area permits us to rule on either their cultural affiliation or the period of occupation. Close by, a shard of pottery of the more recent Late Woodland period, between A.D. 1300 and 1500, was discovered. Is this isolated fragment the detritus of activities connected with the encampment? There can be no certainty, just as it is impossible to say whether the older traces of the encampment on the river-bank are connected with the habitation.

The answers to these questions probably remain sheltered in the cellar of Notre-Dame-de-Bon-Secours Chapel. The researchers have, indeed, left intact certain "archaeological reserves" where, some day, they can continue to follow up the story of this human adventure at the foot of the hillock. For the moment, the first inhabitants continue to keep many of their secrets. Those who succeeded the Amerindians

Prehistory beneath the chapel

For archaeologists, Old Montreal is a place of contrasts. In some places, the ancient soil has been totally destroyed or seriously disturbed by urban construction while, in others, layers of the past are surprisingly well preserved. The archaeological remains of Notre-Dame-de-Bon-Secours Chapel belong to this second category where traces of human presence from a time hundreds of years before the arrival of the Europeans have been found. Some of this archaeological evidence is among the oldest discovered in Old Montreal and, certainly, the only evidence of this era to be displayed on the island of Montreal right at its point of discovery.

What is on display to the public in the archaeological section of the Marguerite Bourgeoys Museum may well be only a tiny portion of the prehistoric "treasures" still sheltered by the site. The archaeological team has, indeed, preserved a large part of the ancient soil without excavating it. About sixty percent of the space of the cellar of the chapel thus constitutes an archaeological reserve where it will eventually be possible to complete the exploration. For example, the area of the Amerindian dwelling place certainly continues under the foundations of the little seventeenth-century chapel, a theory that is plausible since it predates the chapel. So, perhaps the best is yet to come. In fact, in the cellar of the actual chapel, the soil in the whole area to the east of the old chapel is both undisturbed and accessible. We can hope that, one day, this sector will be the subject of new research to determine, among other things, the ethnic identity of the occupants of the dwelling place, their period of occupation and their means of subsistence. Perhaps we shall discover links with the occupations observed at the edge of the embankment a few steps to the south and with those of the neighbouring Accueil Bonneau archaeological site. Exciting discoveries may be in store for the next generation of researchers and of visitors to the museum!

Claude Joyal, archaeologist of prehistory

AMERINDIAN SHARPENING A TOOL

Illustration: Francis Back,
Marguerite Bourgeoys Museum

NOTRE-DAME-DE-BON-SECOURS CHAPEL presented the archaeologists with surprising discoveries. In 1997, Claude Joyal and Pierre-Jacques Ratio discovered a firepit dug about 2000 years ago, intact near the ruins of the little seventeenth-century chapel (in the foreground).

Photograph: Christian Guay,
Marguerite Bourgeoys Museum

in colonizing Montreal have left more obvious traces than their predecessors. Make way for boats, guns, the cross… and lace!

NEW ARRIVALS IN 1642

On a spring day in 1642, in the flower-filled meadow that then bordered the Saint Lawrence, there occurred an event that might have surprised and puzzled the earlier Amerindian inhabitants of the island of Montreal had they been there to witness it. On that day a Mass of thanksgiving was celebrated in the open air. The destiny of the island named Montreal — "*Mont Royal*" — by Jacques Cartier in 1535 had changed forever as, for the first time, Europeans had arrived to make it their home. François Dollier de Casson, the Sulpician historian of Montreal's beginnings, puts their number at fifty-two. Of the group, the names of about forty men and eight women are known, the youngest, Mathurine Godé, only five years old. In the sermon preached to them by the Jesuit missionary Barthélemy Vimont they heard themselves compared to the grain of mustard seed that would grow into a mighty tree. They had embarked on what its organizers saw as a great adventure in faith and its detractors as a "folle entreprise" — a crazy undertaking.

The founding of Ville-Marie on the island of Montreal was a consequence of the great religious renewal in seventeenth-century France that flowed from the reforms of the Council of Trent. The writings of the Jesuit missionaries describing their encounters with the indigenous peoples of the New World had found a large and interested audience in their native France. This audience was not confined to clerics and religious but included many lay persons, especially among their former students and the men and women who came to them for spiritual direction. Among these was Jérôme Le Royer de La Dauversière, a tax collector in La Flèche in the province of Anjou. Although a man of moderate means and the father of at least five children, he was already deeply involved in philanthropic work and founder of a community of nursing nuns, the *Hospitalières de Saint-Joseph*, in his native town.

MEETING OF THE FIRST MEMBERS
OF THE SOCIÉTÉ DE NOTRE-DAME
DE MONTRÉAL, 1640. The four
depicted are Gaston de Renty,
Pierre Chevrier de Fancamp,
Jean-Jacques Olier and Jérôme
Le Royer de La Dauversière.

Louis-Philippe Hébert,
bronze bas-relief, 1895
Place d'Armes, Montreal
Photograph: Rachel Gaudreau,
Marguerite Bourgeoys Museum

In the 1630s, La Dauversière was inspired with the vision of a missionary settlement in New France, a settlement from which the Catholic faith could be preached to the Native Peoples both by word and by example. In the young priest, Jean-Jacques Olier, he met someone who shared his vision. Abbé Olier would soon found the Compagnie de Saint-Sulpice, an association of priests dedicated to the reform of the clergy whose improved education he saw as a most efficacious means of sanctifying the entire Christian people. With Pierre Chevrier, baron de Fancamp, and Baron Gaston de Renty they became the founding members of an association whose object was the establishment of a settlement in New France for the evangelization of the Native Peoples. They were soon to add to their number several other like-minded men and women, many of the men drawn from the membership of the Compagnie du Saint-Sacrement to which the four founders already belonged. The result was the creation of the Société de Notre-Dame de Montréal.

The island of Montreal was chosen as the site for the planned missionary settlement because of its ideal geographical location. According to the *Relations des Jésuites*:

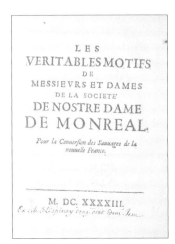

First page of *Les Veritables Motifs de Messieurs et Dames de la Societé de Nostre Dame de Monreal*, published in 1643 to explain the motivation for the founding of Ville-Marie on the island of Montreal.

Bibliothèque centrale de Montréal, Salle Gagnon
Photograph: Christian Poulin, Marguerite Bourgeoys Museum

3. *The Jesuit Relations and Allied Documents: Travels and Explorations of the Jesuit Missionaries in New France, 1610-1791*, ed. Reuben Thwaites, 1898, 22, 207.

[Montreal] gives access and an admirable approach to all the Nations of this vast country; for, on the North and South, on the East and West, there are rivers which fall into the river Saint Lawrence and the river des prairies that surround the Island. So that, if peace prevailed among these peoples, they could land thereon from all sides.[3]

Montreal was at this time uninhabited and the property of Jean de Lauson. In 1640-41 the Société de Notre-Dame bought the island and began definite plans for the establishment of Ville-Marie on the island of Montreal. This involved not only the arrangements for financing the enterprise and the recruitment of suitable settlers but, of key importance, the selection of leaders for the expedition.

The founders of the Société wrote that in answer to the prayers they offered at this juncture, God sent them two leaders, of different sex, condition and place of origin. These were Paul de Chomedey de Maisonneuve and Jeanne Mance. Both were born in the province of Champagne, he on the family estate at Neuville-sur-Vanne and she in Langres in the eastern part of the province.

Paul de Chomedey de Maisonneuve became the first governor of Montreal, responsible for its defence and for the administration of justice. Jeanne Mance was commissioned to establish a hospital. She devoted herself not only to the care of the sick and wounded but also to the organizing of economic aspects of the little colony, to the handling of the common purse and to the distribution of supplies.

The men and women recruited to found Ville-Marie landed at Quebec in 1641, too late to think of establishing themselves on the island of Montreal before the winter. During their sojourn in Quebec they soon discovered how much opposition there was to the founding of a new settlement so far removed from Quebec, given the sparsity of the European population in the Saint Lawrence Valley and the tension between the French and the Iroquois. Maisonneuve, however, in the famous speech put into his mouth by Dollier de Casson, insisted that as he had given his word of honour he would go on to Montreal even "if every tree turned into an Iroquois". Yielding in the face of such determination, Governor Charles Huault de Montmagny

Paul de Chomedey de Maisonneuve

Born at Neuville-sur-Vanne in the province of Champagne, M. de Maisonneuve began his military career at an early age as was the custom of the time. Influenced by contact with the Jesuits, he became a member of the Société de Notre-Dame de Montréal in 1640 and in 1642, the founder and first governor of Ville-Marie. Maisonneuve guided the destiny of the little colony until 1665 when jurisdictional conflicts in New France led to his return to the mother country. He continued to take a lively interest in Montreal and to render what assistance he could, as, for example, in supporting Marguerite Bourgeoys in her quest for letters patent for her community in 1671. When he died in Paris in 1676, the principal bequests in his will were in favour of the Congrégation de Notre-Dame and the Hôtel-Dieu in Montreal.

accompanied the little group up the Saint Lawrence at the beginning of May 1642.

Given the hardships and the dangers confronting them, most of the first settlers recruited for Montreal were men: those who stayed and survived would not marry until they could provide material support for a family. They went to work at once to build a fort which would protect them both from the elements and from their human enemies. The site they chose for the fort had been visited by Champlain thirty years earlier and named Place Royale. Later in the century, Louis-Hector de Callière, who became governor of Montreal in 1684, built his château there and the area took on the name of Pointe à Callière. On the 350th anniversary of Montreal's foundation, the Montréal Museum of History and Archaeology, Pointe-à-Callière, opened on the site.

There were no unpleasant surprises that first summer and, like their human predecessors who had entered the region so long before, the French found the area hospitable. Some of the accounts of those first months sound almost idyllic, those written at the time as well as those in which recollections may have been transformed in the golden

THE FIRST EUROPEAN CEMETERY IN MONTREAL (1643 -1654), next to the fort of Montreal at Pointe à Callière. Seven of the thirty-eight graves were located in 1989. In the foreground of the photo-graph, the only grave unearthed by the archaeologists that still contained a complete skeleton, that of a Frenchman who died at about thirty years of age.

Photograph: Marc Laberge/ Vidéanthrop inc.,
Société du Vieux-Port de Montréal

haze of memory. The *Relations des Jésuites* tell us that on the feast of the Assumption of Mary, 15 August 1642, a great festival was celebrated followed by a procession at which Amerindians were present:

> After the Festival, we visited the great forest which covers this Island; and when we had been led to the mountain from which it takes its name, two of the chief Savages of the band stopped on its summit and told us that they belonged to the nation of those who had formerly dwelt on this Island. Then, stretching out their hands towards the hills that lie to the East and South of the mountain, "There," said they, "are the places where stood Villages filled with great numbers of Savages. The Hurons, who then were our enemies, drove our Forefathers from this country. Some went toward the country of the Abnaquiois, others toward the country of the Hiroquois, some to the Hurons themselves, and joined them. And that is how this Island became deserted." "My grandfather," said an aged man, "tilled the soil on this spot. Maize grew very well on it, for the Sun is very strong there." And, taking in his hands some earth, he said: "See the richness of the soil, it is excellent."[4]

4. *Ibid.*, p. 215.

The speech of these two Algonquin chiefs gives the impression that an Ottawa Valley nation claimed to have previously lived on the island of Montreal. It is not impossible that the orators in the scenario were descendants of the artisans who left their mark just about everywhere in Old Montreal. But the reference to horticulture and thus to the means of subsistence generally associated with Iroquoian people (the Hurons and the Iroquois) seems to contradict the claim of the Algonquin chiefs whose nations were nomadic in nature, hunters, fishers, gatherers. The statement of the two chiefs leads to the supposition that these Algonquins were related in some way to the Saint Lawrence Iroquoians. Is it plausible to see in them descendants of the inhabitants of Hochelaga, a situation resulting from some political event of which we are ignorant?

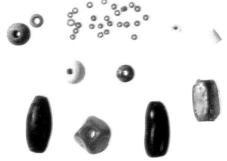

GLASS BEADS USED BY THE FRENCH as currency with the Amerindians in the seventeenth and eighteenth centuries. They were found near the chapel on the Bonsecours site.
Collection of the ministère de la Culture et des Communications du Québec

Photograph: Pierre Fauteux, Ville de Montréal

MONTREAL'S FIRST PILGRIMAGE SITE

In the late autumn of 1642, however, the little colony faced an unexpected danger. The fort was located on a piece of low-lying land at a point where the *rivière* Saint-Pierre flowed into the Saint Lawrence. In December the waters rose so high that the complete inundation of the fort seemed inevitable just as winter was beginning. The response of the first Montrealers to their danger was to pray. They believed that if the establishment of Ville-Marie was really God's will then God would rescue them from the threatened disaster, and they promised that if they were saved they would erect a cross on Mount Royal in gratitude for their deliverance. On Christmas night, the waters began to recede so on 6 January 1643, feast of the Epiphany, the small population accompanied Maisonneuve who carried in liturgical procession what became the first cross on the mountain.

Pilgrimage, the undertaking of a journey to a holy place, was still an important devotional act in seventeenth-century Europe, a form of prayer that involved the participation of the whole body. It was widely practised in the France from which the settlers had come. Now, like the towns and villages of their birth, Montreal had its own pilgrimage destination.

MAISONNEUVE PORTANT UNE
CROIX AU MONT ROYAL - 1643
On 6 January 1643,
Maisonneuve, accompanied by a
solemn procession of the first
Montrealers, carried and erected
the first cross on Mount Royal in
thanksgiving for deliverance from
a flood the previous December.

Stained glass window designed by
Jean-Baptiste Lagacé, Maison Chigot
de Limoges, 1930-31
Basilique Notre-Dame, Montreal
Photograph: © Suzanne Rochette,
1999

THE "YEAR OF THE HUNDRED MEN"

Harrowing years were soon to follow. Although there were no Amerindians living on the island of Montreal at the time of the foundation of Ville-Marie, the settlement was nonetheless very vulnerable to Iroquois attack and the raids that began two years later were to continue with only short periods of peace until the arrival of the Carignan-Salières regiment in 1665. The times were such that those who tried to settle outside the fort, like Jeanne Mance whose first Hôtel-Dieu had been built north-east of the fort by 1645, were frequently forced to seek refuge within its walls. Several of the original settlers left, died or were killed. The recruitment of new settlers was slow and difficult as, indeed, was communication with the members of the Société de Notre-Dame de Montréal in the mother country, although both Maisonneuve and Jeanne Mance made several trips to France for this purpose. The destruction of Huronia in the late 1640s filled all of New France with terror. By 1651, the situation in Ville-Marie, the most exposed of the French settlements, was truly desperate. In the autumn of that year, Maisonneuve left for France convinced that unless he could return with significant reinforcements the "*folle entreprise*" must be entirely abandoned.

To help finance the new recruitment she saw as essential to the survival of the colony, Jeanne Mance put at Maisonneuve's disposal 22,000 *livres* that had been donated by Angélique Faure de Berlise, widow of Claude de Bullion, Treasurer of France, for the establishment of the hospital in Montreal. In exchange, Jeanne Mance received from the seigneury a hundred *arpents* of land for the hospital (this would become the arrière-fief Nazareth). In Paris, Maisonneuve followed the advice of Jeanne Mance and approached her wealthy and generous patron who gave him another 20,000 *livres*. The financial arrangements made at this time were later to cause both Maisonneuve and Jeanne Mance endless trouble but at the moment they undoubtedly saved Montreal. They enabled Maisonneuve to recruit a large enough group of colonists to make 1653 truly a second founding of Montreal, to be remembered always as "the year of the

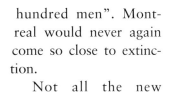

hundred men". Montreal would never again come so close to extinction.

Not all the new Montrealers of 1653 were men. The group also included about fifteen women among whom was Marguerite Bourgeoys whose very presence was an act of confidence in the future of Ville-Marie. In 1649, for the first time, children born in Ville-Marie of French parents survived. It was in his own native Champagne that Maisonneuve found a teacher for them and for the other hoped-for children as yet unborn. Marguerite Bourgeoys was Montreal's first teacher and, some would now say, its first social worker. She would establish, in Montreal, the first religious community of uncloistered women in the New World, a community that, in her lifetime, would welcome Amerindian women among its number. But even before any of these things came to pass, she would become the founder of Notre-Dame-de-Bon-Secours Chapel.

SMALL BOX THAT BELONGED TO MARGUERITE BOURGEOYS. On her departure from France in 1653, Marguerite Bourgeoys took only "a little bundle I could carry under my arm" believing that "if it is God's will, I have no need of anything else." She made three trips back to France and, on her second voyage (1670-1672) to seek letters patent for the Congrégation de Notre-Dame, she left Montreal with "a box containing my clothing and my blanket." This box was missing when she reached Quebec. When it was found, the papers were sent after her on the next ship but the box was returned to Montreal.

Still-born calf skin, lock and handle added in the eighteenth century

Photograph: Bernard Dubois, Marguerite Bourgeoys Museum

CHAPTER TWO

MONTREAL'S FIRST STONE CHURCH (1655-1754)

MARGUERITE BOURGEOYS was to wait five years before she could open the first school in Montreal. Meanwhile, she lived in the fort and directed the governor's household. She went from house to house teaching the women to read and accepted the care of both the first children to survive and the young women recruited by the Société de Notre-Dame de Montréal as prospective wives for the settlers. Even before she reached Montreal, Maisonneuve had told her about the cross on the mountain, Montreal's first pilgrimage site, and one of her first acts on arrival was to oversee a work party to once again raise the cross that had been overthrown in the interim. But the constant danger of Iroquois attack soon made pilgrimage to the cross too dangerous and Marguerite began to think of another pilgrimage site closer to the fort, a site that, like many in her native France, would be dedicated to the Blessed Virgin Mary.

A CHAPEL FOR MARY IN VILLE-MARIE

What year was this chapel begun? This is not an easy question to answer. Marie Morin, the annalist of the Hôtel-Dieu de Montréal and a long-time friend of Marguerite Bourgeoys says that Marguerite conceived the idea of building a chapel of pilgrimage dedicated to Mary two years after her arrival in Ville-Marie, and she specifies the year, 1655. Although 1657 is the date traditionally given for the foundation of the chapel, if, as is usually held, M. de Maisonneuve granted the land for the chapel in the name of the Société de Notre-Dame de

Montréal, he must have done so at an earlier date. The governor left Montreal for France in the autumn of 1655 and did not return until August 1657 when work on the chapel was, apparently, already underway.

Until the summer of 1657 Montreal was a mission served by the Jesuits. From the very beginning, Ville-Marie was destined by its founders to have a parish church dedicated to Mary, but the settlers worshipped at first in the chapel of the fort then, from 1654, in the chapel of the Hôtel-Dieu dedicated to Saint Joseph. Marguerite obtained approval for the construction of the chapel of pilgrimage from Father Claude Pijart, the Jesuit missionary who also chose its name, Notre-Dame-de-Bon-Secours, Our Lady of Good Help, a title which must have seemed very apt in the perilous conditions of the time.

Marguerite Bourgeoys also tells us: "Father Le Moyne placed the first stone. M. Closse had the necessary inscription engraved on a copper plate and the masons began their work." Her next words are, "But that same year, Monsieur de Queylus arrived in Québec …", an event that, as we shall see below, took place in 1657. The role played by Lambert Closse, Maisonneuve's deputy, would suggest that the first stone was laid between 1655 and 1657 during the governor's absence. The Father Le Moyne to whom Marguerite refers was Simon Le Moyne, one of the Jesuit missionaries most valued for his work among the Amerindians. At about this time, Father Le Moyne made three important trips to the Iroquois country as an ambassador of peace, one in 1655, one in 1656 and one in 1657-58. On each of these trips he passed through Montreal. On which of these might he have laid the first stone for the chapel? That of 1657-58 when he did not leave Quebec until 26 August would have been too late, for by that time Montreal was no longer a Jesuit mission. When Marguerite Bourgeoys spoke of the "same year", was she perhaps thinking not in terms of the calendar year but, like Dollier de Casson in his *Histoire du Montréal*, of the interval between the departure of the ships for France each autumn? In such a case, the first stone might have been laid when Father Le Moyne was in Montreal in the autumn of 1656.

It is certain that the building of the chapel was a task that involved the whole settlement. One of the greatest gifts Marguerite Bourgeoys brought with her to Montreal was her ability to create a spirit of community and she immediately displayed it in the manner in which she inspired the construction of the chapel. She wrote:

> I urged the few people who were here at the time to gather stone. I used to do sewing and in payment, I asked for a day's work. I collected alms to pay for the masons' work. M. de Maisonneuve had the necessary timber squared. Others prepared the lime, the sand and the boards and soon I had found enough [material] to build it and roof it.

Neither Marguerite Bourgeoys nor Marie Morin, the two contemporary witnesses who tell us most about the chapel, gives any description of the site chosen but the archaeological excavations of 1997-98 and certain old maps throw some light on the subject.

POSTPONED BUT NOT ABANDONED

Although materials for the building of the chapel were collected and the foundation laid, the moment for its actual construction had not yet arrived. Maisonneuve's 1655 voyage to France was, in great part, to seek replacements for the Jesuits who had indicated that they could not continue to guarantee the presence of their missionaries in Ville-Marie. When the governor returned in the summer of 1657, he was accompanied by four Sulpicians who arrived with the intention of transforming Montreal from mission to parish. Sending these priests to Montreal was the last gesture of support for the colony made by M. Olier who died as the four awaited departure. When Marguerite Bourgeoys sought permission to continue work on the chapel from Gabriel Thubières de Levy de Queylus, the superior of the newly arrived group, he ordered the work suspended. It was to remain so for more than a decade while the ecclesiastical authorities of New France were caught up in the jurisdictional disputes that were to last for the next several years.

The life of Marguerite Bourgeoys was also undergoing significant change at this time. Before her departure from France, Marguerite

MARGUERITE BOURGEOYS ARRIVES IN VILLE-MARIE.

Illustration: Francis Back; Marguerite Bourgeoys Museum

STAIRCASE FROM THE BOURGEOYS' FAMILY HOME IN TROYES. When the Bourgeoys family home was demolished in 1976, the city of Troyes salvaged parts of one of the staircases. A group of apprentice carpenters restored the staircase and gave it to the Congrégation de Notre-Dame. One section remained in Troyes at the Centre culturel Marguerite-Bourgeoys and the other was sent to Montreal. This sixteenth-century staircase is now the symbol of a common past uniting the cities of Troyes and Montreal.

Photograph: Rachel Gaudreau, Marguerite Bourgeoys Museum

had been part of an attempt to bring into being a new kind of religious life for women. At that time, religious life for women meant the cloister, not only for contemplatives but also for those involved in apostolic activity. The cloister restricted their contact with the outside world and in a special way with the poor. Marguerite's spiritual director in Troyes, Father Antoine Gendret, had told her that, while Saint Mary Magdalen was the model of contemplative women religious and Saint Martha of cloistered religious who also performed some apostolic activity, there was a third alternative model, the Blessed Virgin Mary. Marguerite saw in Mary, the mother of Jesus, the possiblity that without cloister, wimple or veil one could be a "true religious" living, working and teaching alongside other Christians as Mary had done in the early Christian church. Marguerite's first attempt to participate in such a community failed when, of two companions, one died and one married. Before she came to Montreal, Marguerite had already pronounced private vows of poverty, chastity and obedience and, although she had to come alone, she had not abandoned the hope that "what God had not willed in Troyes He would bring to pass in Montreal."

In January 1658, Maisonneuve deeded to Marguerite Bourgeoys a stone building on the common, a piece of communal grazing land east of the fort, still recalled in the name of *rue* de la Commune. The building had served as a stable until the herdsman, Antoine Roos, was killed by the Iroquois in 1652. A plaque at the south-west corner of the present Saint-Paul and Saint-Dizier streets indicates the spot where Marguerite Bourgeoys opened Montreal's first school on 30 April 1658.

Both Marguerite Bourgeoys and Jeanne Mance now felt ready to seek out other women to help with the work each had begun in Ville-Marie. In September 1658, the two left for France. When they returned a year later, Jeanne Mance was accompanied by three nuns from the community founded by Jérôme Le Royer de La Dauversière in La Flèche. Marguerite Bourgeoys had found four companions who contracted to live in community and help with the work of teaching

Troyes, capital of Champagne

Troyes, city of merchants and poets, was the capital of Champagne, the native province of Paul de Chomedey de Maisonneuve, Jeanne Mance and Marguerite Bourgeoys. It traced its origins to Roman times and because of its location on the main trade routes became an important centre of commerce in the middle ages when travellers from all over the known world rubbed shoulders in its market place. Medieval Troyes was also a city of romance and learning, associated with Chrétien de Troyes, the poet of courtly love, and Rachi of Troyes, the great Jewish scholar. Its many beautiful churches may have helped inspire in Marguerite Bourgeoys the desire to erect a Marian chapel in Ville-Marie.

MARGUERITE BOURGEOYS WAS BORN in the second house to the left where her father, Abraham Bourgeoys, conducted his candle-making business. The house was demolished in 1976.

Photograph: Armour Landry, 1950. Archives nationales du Québec, P97

the daughters of both the French settlers and the Amerindians. Three of these women were to remain with Marguerite permanently. Although both civil and ecclesiastical recognition lay in the future, this group was, in fact, the nucleus of the Congrégation de Notre-Dame de Montréal, an uncloistered community of women able to move freely among the people in their work of education. Beginning in the early 1660s, legal documents in Montreal refer to the stable-school as the "Maison de la Congrégation". But a sad disappointment awaited Marguerite on her return to Montreal: "I found the materials that had been collected for the chapel all scattered."

In the next few years, Marguerite Bourgeoys was absorbed by the growth of her educational work which extended far beyond the instruction of the children. Because she believed "we must open wide the doors of the Blessed Virgin's house to all young women", she also welcomed into her household the *filles du Roi* who began to arrive in Montreal in 1663. The Congregation and its work soon outgrew the former stable and any material resources the group possessed had to be devoted to the building of larger quarters. But Marguerite never forgot the chapel: "I used to pray to the Blessed Virgin and to promise her that I would build her chapel."

In 1670, Marguerite Bourgeoys made another trip to France to obtain the civil charter for her community and to recruit more companions. Before she left Montreal, she had a wooden structure erected on the site of the chapel, a structure she refers to as a "charpente" (framework) and Marie Morin calls "un petit bâtiment de bois" (a little wooden building). The 1675 deliberations of the wardens of Notre-Dame parish were to describe this building as "a small wooden building in the form of a chapel, about four hundred paces from Ville-Marie ... raised on an old foundation built by ... Marguerite Bourgeoys ten years earlier."

A MADONNA FOR THE CHAPEL

Marguerite Bourgeoys did not forget the chapel during her stay in France. Although the Société de Notre-Dame had ceased to exist and the Sulpicians had become seigneurs of the island of Montreal in 1663, it is apparent that some of those who had been its members continued to take an interest in the project they had initiated. When the Baron de Fancamp offered to help defray the expenses of her trip, Marguerite asked instead for a gift for the chapel. He gave her a statuette of Virgin and Child about 15 centimetres in height, a work that already had a remarkable history. Carved from the oak of Montaigu, a renowned place of Marian pilgrimage in Belgium, the statuette was presented to Pierre de Fancamp by the barons Denys et Louis le Prêtre who had also belonged to the Société de Notre-Dame de Montréal. The brothers testified that the statuette had been left to them by their mother when she died at the age of more than eighty years, that it was more than one hundred years old and that it had been kept in their family chapel. During the time it was in his possession, the Baron de Fancamp believed he had been miraculously cured of a serious illness. In addition to the statuette, he also gave a gift of money for the enlargement or decoration of the chapel, 300 *livres* according to Marie Morin. In 1672 Marguerite Bourgeoys brought the statuette to Montreal where it was first kept in the house of the Congregation. On 8 June 1673 the statuette was placed in the little

STATUETTE OF VIRGIN AND CHILD in oak, described in documents as "wooden image of Notre Dame de Montaigu", given to Marguerite Bourgeoys for the chapel by the Baron de Fancamp in 1672. Now known as Notre-Dame-de-Bon-Secours and exhibited on the left side-altar of the chapel. Photograph: Rachel Gaudreau, Marguerite Bourgeoys Museum

Pierre Chevrier, baron de Fancamp

Born in Paris, Pierre Chevrier de Fancamp studied at the Jesuit college in La Flèche where he became the close friend of Jérôme Le Royer de La Dauversière, a member of the Compagnie du Saint Sacrement and one of the founding members of the Société de Notre-Dame de Montréal. He was ordained to the priesthood in 1652. In the official acts naming the seigneurs of Montreal from August 1640 to 1663, the name of the baron de Fancamp heads the list because his superior wealth and social position made him a more acceptable guarantor than Le Royer. He continued to take an interest in Montreal even after the death of his friend and the disappearance of the Société de Notre-Dame. In 1672, he

MOSAIC OF PIERRE CHEVRIER DE FANCAMP after a drawing by Annette Joubert, 1958

Photograph: Rachel Gaudreau, Marguerite Bourgeoys Museum

presented Marguerite Bourgeoys with the miraculous statuette of Notre-Dame-de-Bon-Secours and contributed financially to the building of the chapel. He also continued to give generous financial help to the Hôtel-Dieu in Montreal. Pierre Chevrier, baron de Fancamp, died in Paris in June 1692.

wooden building on the site of the chapel. The same precious object, the gift of the Baron de Fancamp more than three centuries ago, can still be seen in Notre-Dame-de-Bon-Secours-Chapel.

MONTREAL'S FIRST STONE CHURCH

In a letter dated 24 August 1673 Jean Dudouyt, Vicar General to Bishop Laval, gave permission for work on the chapel to continue, although, since it was to be a place of pilgrimage, he expressed a preference for a site further away from Ville-Marie. Apparently his view did not prevail for Marie Morin expressly states that the chapel was built on the site where the original foundations had been laid. On 4 November 1674, Henri de Bernières, Vicar General, wrote to Marguerite Bourgeoys approving the choice of Mary in the mystery of her

IT IS POSSIBLE TO PICTURE THE CHAPEL IN ITS NATURAL SETTING thanks to archaeological discoveries and to computer-assisted projections. This hypothetical reconstruction of the area in about 1680 is based on archaeological evidence (dimensions, shape and position of the chapel, building materials, unevenness of the terrain, the road in front) and on historical documents (shape and position of the steeple, fenestration, the road in front).

Virtual historic reconstruction: Omar Bakar, GRAPH Architecture inc., Marguerite Bourgeoys Museum

LEAD COMMEMORA-TIVE PLAQUE placed under the first stone in the foundation of Notre-Dame-de-Bon-Secours Chapel in the centre of the apse, 30 June 1675.

BRASS ENGRAVING WITH IMAGE OF VIRGIN AND CHILD, described in the texts as "copper medal of the Blessed Virgin", placed with the commemorative plaque, in 1675.

These objects were recovered after the 1754 fire and placed with the commemorative plaque of the 1771 chapel. The three objects were rediscovered in 1945 when the centre of the wall of the crypt in the apse was pierced to provide an exit on *rue de la Commune*.

Photographs: Pierre Fauteux, Marguerite Bourgeoys Museum

Assumption into heaven as the titulary of the chapel. After vespers on 29 June 1675, a procession wended its way to plant a cross at the site of the chapel and the preparatory work began. The next day at the same hour, another procession accompanied the Sulpician Gabriel Souart as he laid the first stone in the name of the Baron de Fancamp. Beneath this stone were placed a lead plaque bearing the inscription "*D O M et Beata Maria Virgini Sub Titulo Assumptionis ...*" with a copper medal of the Blessed Virgin.

Marie Morin says funds for the building of the chapel came from the Congrégation de Notre-Dame (the document annexing the chapel to the parish specifies that the Congregation had advanced 2400 *livres*) and from the gift of the Baron de Fancamp invested by Marguerite Bourgeoys. The Sulpicians also gave their financial help to the chapel. In addition, M. Souart paid for the casting of a bell from a broken cannon given earlier by Maisonneuve, and Dollier de Casson gave the chapel the stipends from all the masses that would be said

THE RUINS OF MONTREAL'S FIRST STONE CHURCH seen from the façade. Although the main body was constructed of field stone, rather than quarried stone, the corners of the building are in cut stone to ensure its stability.

Photograph: Pierre Fauteux, Ville de Montréal

Notre-Dame-de-Bonsecours and the old Citadel of Montreal, watercolour by James Duncan about 1845.

Musée de la civilisation, collection of the Séminaire de Québec no. 1993-15078

WHAT WAS THE CHAPEL REALLY LIKE? Contemporary representations of the first Notre-Dame-de-Bon-Secours Chapel are very rare. In the mid-1800s, at the request of Jacques Viger, the artist James Duncan illustrated the chapel as he imagined it from reading old maps: isolated from the town, small, with its steeple above the façade. Today we know that the steeple was built in the centre of the building as seen in the other two illustrations. This tradition disappeared at the end of the seventeenth century.

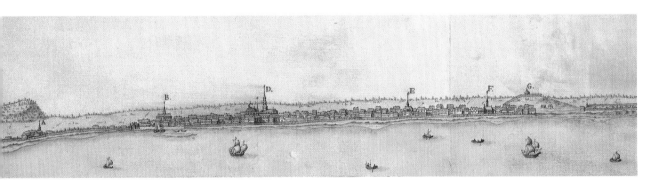

Extract from "Veue de la Ville du Montréal en Canada," circa 1720. The letter F marks the chapel.

Edward E. Ayer Collection, The Newberry Library, Chicago

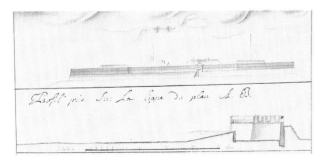

Outline drawing of the fortifications of Montreal seen from the Quebec Gate, done by the Montreal surveyor René de Couagne in 1749; from this angle, the central steeple of Notre-Dame-de-Bon-Secours is clearly visible.

Centre des Archives d'Outre-Mer, Aix-en-Provence (A.N.France) DFC Amérique septentrionale no. 488A

Montreal's First Stone Church ❀ 43

there for the next three years. Marguerite Bourgeoys wrote that there were more than a thousand Masses "although there were few priests and few people in Montreal." (The population of Ville-Marie in 1678 was less than 700; that of the island of Montreal reached the number of 1322 in 1680). The numbers cited by Marguerite Bourgeoys would suggest that mass was celebrated in the chapel almost every day. Certainly the *Délibérations de la fabrique de la Paroisse de Notre-Dame de Ville-Marie* state that by the middle of the eighteenth century, mass was celebrated daily in the chapel.

That the Congregation was also called upon to give more than financial help in the building of the chapel is demonstrated by the following incident recorded by Marguerite Bourgeoys:

> When the masons were building the steps at the door, we had a hired man who was not willing to go and help the masons. At that time, Sister Sommillard had an abscess in the head from which she suffered so much that she was unable to bend over; she was even obliged to kneel when she wanted to sweep her room. Nevertheless, she went to work at once

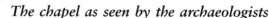

The chapel as seen by the archaeologists

An archaeological discovery is ordinarily the result of an informed mixture of planning and hard work, of good luck and sometimes inexplicable coincidences. That is what we, the archaeologists in charge of the dig during the restoration of Notre-Dame-de-Bon-Secours Chapel and the Marguerite Bourgeoys Museum, now believe in light of our fortunate discoveries. For, in this instance, armed with a certain theoretical knowledge of the site to be assessed, we had the good fortune to discover the hoped-for jewel from the very outset of the work. This good fortune was apparent in the results of a test trench in the cellar of the present nave at the end of 1997. From that moment, we were able to confirm that the remains of the 1675 chapel were well and truly preserved there. Under the diffused lighting of our electric lamps, we were able to discern a small section of foundation rubble stone held together with mortar, forming a gradual curve on its outer surface. This vestige lay beside an accumulation of layers of ancient soils revealing a long human occupation of the site, from the Amerindian origins to our own day. From that decisive moment in our operations, a series of discoveries yielded one of the rare archaeological collections of Old Montreal dating from the origins of Ville-Marie.

But test trenches offer only a partial and limited reading of a site. To continue our research, we had to show the importance of our discoveries in the context of the remodeling of the Marguerite Bourgeoys Museum and their eventual integration into the museum plan. The cooperation of the Sisters of the Congrégation de Notre-Dame, of the Priests of Saint-Sulpice and of the architect of the project allowed us to excavate an open area and to uncover an exceptional archaeological site, that of Montreal's first stone chapel founded by Marguerite Bourgeoys. When the chapel was demolished after the 1754 fire, only the foundations were left intact. It was the leveled crest of these that we had uncovered, providing precious information on the dimensions of the

BEFORE: THE CELLAR OF NOTRE-DAME-DE-BON-SECOURS IN 1996 before the archaeological dig.

AFTER: THE RUINS OF THE BURNED CHAPEL as discovered by the archaeologists beneath the present chapel. In the sanctuary are the three low walls (the base of the altar steps?), the base of the altar in the background and the curve of the apse. The stone cross was part of the façade of the second chapel from 1771-1892.

Photographs: Pierre Fauteux, Ville de Montréal

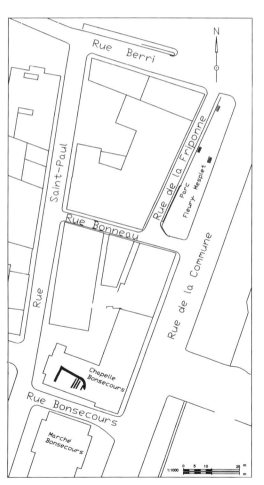

PLAN of the archaeological remains of the first chapel.

Plan: François Véronneau, Groupe de recherches en histoire du Québec, Marguerite Bourgeoys Museum

Montreal's First Stone Church ❖ 45

building — about 14 by 8 metres — and on the remains preserved in the cellar of the present church built in 1771. The excavation of the interior of the apse and of part of the original nave revealed, under the debris, the layer from the devastating fire containing pieces of burned wood, architectural hardware and melted glass, evidence of the intensity of the inferno. Also, we uncovered a series of three low, parallel walls in masonry, then a fourth almost right against the apse wall. What was their function? The wall against the apse probably supported the altar. As for the other three low walls, we noticed that the level of the fire that separated them rose continually as it neared the altar. This gradual ascension led to the hypothesis that these three walls served as the base of the altar steps.

Beside the façade outside the building, we disengaged the remains of pieces of charred wood laid flat on the earth with four traces of stakes that confirmed the presence of the porch at the main entrance, as illustrated in some ancient plans. To the east, on the side of the only lateral wall still intact, emerged, at last, beneath the rubble of occupation accumulated over time, the remains of stakes from the wooden stockade. This section joined to the apse corresponded to the extension of the palisade surrounding the town in 1709. The stakes were, we believe, physical evidence of the line demarcating the fortified town observed in the plan produced by Gédéon de Catalogne in 1713. Not everything was revealed in the course of the excavations — far from it — and many questions remain. About two thirds of the interior area of the little chapel has not been excavated and none of the earth beneath the level of the fire has been dug. Does this archaeological reserve contain, as we believe, the graves of the hospital sisters buried beneath the chapel in 1734? Does it preserve traces of earlier occupation related to the time when Marguerite Bourgeoys and her fellow citizens came in pilgrimage to the chapel? Will we find there, beneath the ruins of the 1675 chapel, traces of the original project unfinished in the summer of 1657? Only extensive excavations would provide answers to these questions. And probably raise new ones ...

François Véronneau and Pierre-Jacques Ratio, archaeologists
Groupe de recherches en histoire du Québec

and helped the masons for two or three hours with all the strength of a man and without even thinking of her condition. It should be noted that from that moment, she felt no more pain for a whole year.

The chapel, Montreal's first stone church, was completed in 1678 and the statuette given by the Baron de Fancamp was placed there for the veneration of the faithful.

In November 1678, with the approval of Bishop Laval, the chapel was ceded to Notre-Dame Parish to which it would be annexed "in perpetuity" although the document specifies that the sisters of the Congregation would continue to take care of it in the future as they had done in the past. Marguerite Bourgeoys herself wrote that "many marvels were accomplished by the prayers that were said in this chapel" and at the end of the century Marie Morin wrote that "the people went there as to a certain refuge in all their needs." She added that the chapel was the site of many cures believed to be miraculous "as much for the soul, for the strength and courage obtained from God to turn away from sin, as for the body through the healing of many serious illnesses."

The chapel continued to play an important role in the life of Marguerite Bourgeoys and her Congregation. Despite some setbacks, like the fire of 6 December 1683 that devastated the "*Grand' Maison*", the larger house built in the early 1670s when the stable-school had become inadequate to the needs of the Congregation, the community continued to grow. In 1669, Bishop Laval had approved the "*Filles séculières de Ville-Marie*" and authorized them to teach wherever they were invited in his diocese, which covered the whole of New France. In addition to the "travelling missions" (*missions ambulantes*) they had undertaken from the early 1660s, their farmhouse at Pointe Saint-Charles (1668) and their work at the Mountain Mission for Amerindians in Montreal (1676), the sisters of the Congregation went out, mostly two by two, to open schools in Champlain (1676), Pointe-aux-Trembles, Montreal (1678), Lachine (1680), Sault Saint-Louis (Amerindian mission, 1683), Sainte-Famille, Île d'Orléans (1685), Château-Richer (1689) and Quebec Lower Town (1692).

HOLY WATER FONT in glazed earthenware discovered on the archaeological site of the chapel, (seventeenth century or first half of the eighteenth century). Note the repair holes along the breaks.

Collection of the ministère de la Culture et des Communications du Québec
Photograph: Pierre Fauteux, Ville de Montréal

Reflecting the growth and perhaps the diversity of the population of Montreal in the last quarter of the seventeenth century, the Congregation that had begun with a tiny group of French women, largely from Marguerite's native Champagne, came to include "*Canadiennes*", two Amerindian women and even two women from the English colonies. Brought to Montreal as captives of the Amerindian

Marguerite Bourgeoys
Born in Troyes, the capital city of Champagne, Marguerite Bourgeoys decided in 1640, at the age of twenty, to give her life to God. When she was rejected by the cloistered communities of her time, she worked among the poor of Troyes for thirteen years as a member of an extern group associated with the Congrégation de Notre-Dame of Troyes, itself a cloistered teaching community of women. This led Louise de Chomedey de Sainte-Marie, the director of the extern group, to suggest Marguerite's name to her brother Paul as a teacher for Ville-Marie. Marguerite arrived in Ville-Marie in 1653. There she founded one of the first uncloistered communities of women in the Catholic Church, a community that in her own time included Amerindians and women from the English colonies alongside women from France and the daughters of the first settlers. These women taught not only on the island of Montreal but also in Trois-Rivières, Quebec and in the little settlements along the Saint Lawrence. Marguerite founded Notre-Dame-de-Bon-Secours Chapel, welcomed the "filles du Roi" and generally helped the early settlers in all their needs. She died in Montreal in 1700 and was buried in the first Notre-Dame Church on 13 January, the day after her death. Generally regarded as a saint at the time of her death, she was canonized in 1982.

LE « VRAI PORTRAIT » DE MARGUERITE BOURGEOYS. This work is the only known likeness of the real face of Marguerite Bourgeoys. Painted by Pierre Le Ber immediately after her death, 12 January 1700, it is the oldest existing painting by an artist born in Canada. Contempt for its primitive and austere style led to the superimposition of another image of Margurite Bourgeoys on the canvas in the middle of the nineteenth century. This was removed and the painting restored in 1963.

Pierre LeBer, oil on canvas; Marguerite Bourgeoys Museum

allies, these women elected to remain there and to join the Congregation. So, among the names of the sisters of the Congrégation de Notre-Dame in the seventeenth century are found not only Raisin and Sommillard but Barbier and Le Moyne, Attontinon and Gannensagouas, Longley and Sayward. And all these women must have frequented the little chapel for it was there that the Congregation always celebrated its patronal feast and there, Marguerite wrote, that "we always renewed the promises we had made to God." By the time of her death in Montreal on 12 January 1700, Marguerite Bourgeoys would have seen great changes both in her Congregation and in the tiny colony to which she had come almost fifty years earlier. There is no doubt that part of the development was due to the existence of Notre-Dame-de-Bon-Secours Chapel.

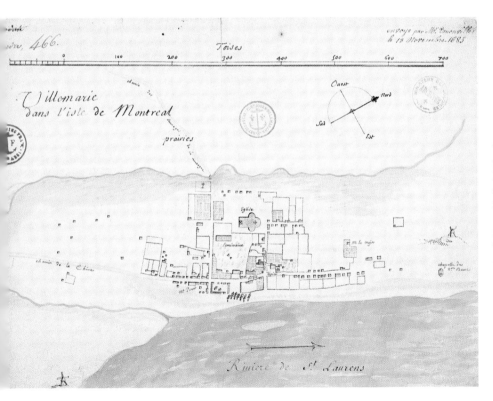

VILLE-MARIE IN 1685. That year, the governor general of New France, Jacques-René de Brisay de Denonville, wrote to the minister of the navy in France: "In Montreal, I found gunpowder in the top of a little chapel to which the population was greatly devoted. The bishop made a serious plea to have it removed but, without another place to store it safe from the danger of fire, I was unable to comply." Sketch attributed to the engineer Robert de Villeneuve.

Centre des Archives d'Outre-Mer, Aix-en-Provence (A.N.France) DFC Amérique septentrionale no. 466C

BONSECOURS, A *FAUBOURG* OF CRAFTSMEN

The annexation of the chapel to the parish seemed like a sign of the imminent expansion of the town. Of all the *faubourgs* of Montreal that were to grow up around the town core, Bonsecours was the first. The reassuring presence of the chapel and of the faithful who visited it daily provided good reason for Montrealers to settle in this neighbourhood. Even so, it would be a good quarter of a century before the *faubourg* Bonsecours took shape and developed an identity of its own. During this period, the Sulpician Dollier de Casson gradually offered several Montrealers land grants in the area between the town limits, then around what is now Place Jacques-Cartier, and the chapel. But the shaping of the district was also directly affected by the defence requirements of the town. Changes to the layout of the 1689 palisade and the construction of stone fortifications between 1717 and 1740 would several times transform the principal means of access to the town and, hence, the streets and land divisions of the neighbourhood.

In 1687, the year that the authorities began to fortify the town to protect it from attack by the Iroquois, all of the lands west of Bonsecours had been granted although not all the sites were inhabited yet. Despite the seigneurial rule requiring owners to set up hearth and home on their grant, few of the new arrivals had the means to establish themselves quickly. The sparse population of the area did not warrant its inclusion within the first wooden palisade of the town even though the chapel was used as a makeshift powder magazine. Neither the hill nor the house established by the Jesuits on their return in 1692 was within the first enclosure although both were close to the town. Moreover, the merchant elite showed little liking for this district, no doubt too far removed from the business centre. No matter! Snubbed by the major tradesmen, the *faubourg* Bonsecours had become the stronghold of craftsmen, as illustrated in the accompanying table of occupations.

These proportions contrast with those characteristic of the same sectors of activity in the town as a whole. The historian Louise Dechêne estimates that, in the Montreal of 1715, the service sector

OCCUPANTS AND OWNERS IN THE *faubourg* BONSECOURS BY SECTOR OF ACTIVITY BETWEEN 1675 AND 1700[1]		
Services	5 (9%)	4 military officers
		1 justice officer
Trade	8 (15%)	1 outfitter
		2 voyageurs & small business owners
		2 bakers & butchers
Secondary sector (manufacturers)		
	24 (45%)	12 building craftsmen (carpenters, masons, cabinetmakers)
		4 iron craftsmen (tool makers, coppersmiths)
		3 shoemakers
		1 sabot maker
		1 candlemaker
Farmers	11 (20%)	
Other	1 (2%)	1 soldier
Occupation unknown	5 (9%)	
TOTAL	54 (100%)	

1. These statistics were compiled from the Adhémar database (Research group on Montreal, Canadian Centre for Architecture) and from seventeenth-century notarial acts.

occupied about 40% of the population and that of production, about 25%. Like the vast majority of dwellings in the town, the houses of the craftsmen and farmers of the *faubourg* were single-storey, wooden *pièces-sur-pièces* homes. The living area was usually modest in size and occasionally there were also outbuildings. Although most of the owners were residents, others rented out their houses, exacting payment in cash or in kind. Some owners, for example, demanded half the manure produced by the tenants' animals! In the absence of cash, the barter system was a widely-used substitute. The surveyor and engineer Gédéon de Catalogne resorted to bartering when he leased the sand from his sandpit in the *faubourg* for a period of nine years to the masons Jean-Baptiste and Jacques Tessier in exchange for the yearly delivery of four cords of wood.

PINS AND 1692 COIN FOUND AT NOTRE-DAME-DE-BON-SECOURS. In 1689, the carpenter Léonard Paillé, *dit* Paillard, hired René Alary to build him a house in the *faubourg* Bonsecours. According to a custom already in decline, he paid Alary 400 *livres* in silver and 10 *livres* in pins payable to his wife. Perhaps one of these pins was used to hold up the hem of Madame Alary's dress when she came to the chapel to pray.

Collection of the ministère de la Culture et des Communications du Québec.

Photographs: Pierre Fauteux, Marguerite Bourgeoys Museum (above) Ville de Montréal (below)

Marie Brazeau

One of the first neighbours of Notre-Dame-de-Bon-Secours Chapel was Marie Brazeau who was born in Paris around 1662. She married Sylvain Guérin in Amboise (Touraine) on 30 October 1679. Two years later, the entire Brazeau family emigrated to New France: Nicolas Brazeau and Perrine Billard, his wife, and their two sons, Nicolas and Charles, as well as Marie and her one year-old child. Sylvain Guérin did not make the voyage at this time but joined his wife in 1685. For some unknown reason, he returned to France in 1688 after the birth of their third child, never again to return to New France.

Abandoned by her husband, Marie Brazeau obtained the concession of a piece of land on the north-east corner of the present Bonsecours

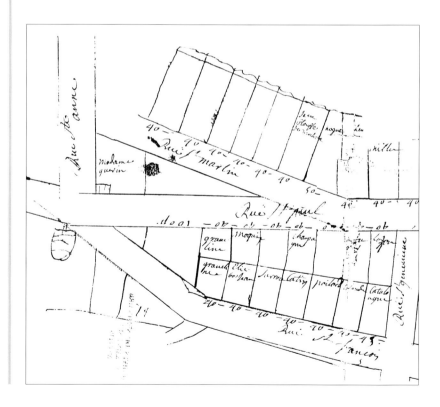

THE *FAUBOURG* BONSECOURS. On this 17th century plan the names of several residents of the district can be seen, among them "Madame guerin", that is, Marie Brazeau, the wife of Sylvain Guérin. In 1698, she married Guillaume Tougard known as Laviolette. the Chapel can be seen on the left.

Archives of the Séminaire de Saint-Sulpice, Montreal.

and Saint-Paul streets. On this site, she had a house built "opposite Notre-Dame-de-Bon-Secours Chapel." This house belonging to "Madame guérin" is clearly indicated on an undated plan probably drawn before 1693. To survive, Marie Brazeau set up a tavern in her house. A regular customer, Antoine Beaujean, soon became her lover. In 1691, after the birth of a child whom he refused to acknowledge as his, Antoine, well known for his penchant for fast living, dropped out of sight for a while, scared off perhaps by the rumours circulating that Sylvain Guérin had been hanged for bigamy in Amboise. He returned, however, to hang around the cabaret of the forsaken wife in 1692, and Marie Brazeau became pregnant once more. Despite all of his fine promises of marriage, Antoine abandoned Marie who took him to court to obtain compensation. Marie won her case but it was a bittersweet victory since Antoine was killed by the Iroquois in 1693. In 1695, Marie Brazeau gave birth to a girl, "the natural child of an unknown man." Outraged by the situation, Nicolas Brazeau disinherited his daughter.

Then, into her life came a young soldier, twenty-four years of age, Guillaume Tougard, known as Laviolette, who married her in November 1698. Marie was literally transformed into a model wife and caring mother. Once again in the good graces of her father, Marie bore six children to Guillaume Tougard who became a cartwright like his father-in-law and worked a piece of land as well at côte Saint-Michel. He died prematurely in September 1708. In 1712, Marie Brazeau was married again, this time to Didier Bourgouin who died shortly after. She then married Pierre Tastet known as Francoeur in 1713. Marie Brazeau died a septuagenarian on 29 May 1735 after having lived more than forty years in the *faubourg* Bonsecours.

The little *pièce-sur-pièce* house so long occupied by the Tougards and the Brazeaus opposite the chapel at the corner of Saint-Paul and Bonsecours measured twenty-two by eighteen French feet and was covered in planks. On the same spot today stands the Maison du Calvet, built around 1770.

Rémi Tougas, eng.
Ninth generation descendant
of Guillaume Tougard
and Marie Brazeau

SIGNATURE DE MARIE BRAZEAU

A number of family "dynasties" that lasted for several generations were established in the district. The Brazeau, Demers, Testard and Viger families were among the most prominent residents. Nicolas Brazeau, master wheelwright, taught the trade to his sons, Nicolas and Charles. Their sister, Marie, settled close to the family property after a first marriage to the shoemaker, Sylvain Guérin. Nearby, the farmer André Demers saw two of his children, Jean-Baptiste and André, settle close to the chapel to practise their trade as tool-makers. The Viger family specialized in shoemaking and carpentry. On another note, the presence of military officers Jacques Testard de Montigny and his older brother Gabriel Testard de LaForest, sons of a rich merchant, offered a contrast to this world of craftsmen and farmers.

MONTREAL IN 1713. On this plan drawn by Gédéon de Catalogne, the Bonsecours district has been included within the town limits. The apse of Notre-Dame-de-Bon-Secours is an integral part of the fortifications. On either side of the chapel are the imposing residences of Charles Le Moyne de Longueuil and of Jacques Testard de Montigny.

Ministère de la défense, France - Service historique de l'armée de terre - Génie, Article 14, Montréal

We shall never know what reason prompted the Testard brothers, at the time in their early twenties, to acquire two adjoining sites east of Notre-Dame-de-Bon-Secours in 1682. We do know, however, that the younger of the two, Testard de Montigny, had the terms of his grant altered in 1693 to permit immediate construction next to the chapel. It is likely that his presence at this precise moment was related to more recent political events in the colony that would have a profound impact on the urban development of the *faubourg*.

In 1690, war had broken out between France and England. Made vulnerable by a poor defence system, Montreal became a potential target for the neighbouring English colonies. As partial remedy for this situation, Governor Callière fortified the famous hill that over-

Jacques Testard de Montigny about 1715; 19th-century portrait
Collection of
Château Ramezay Museum

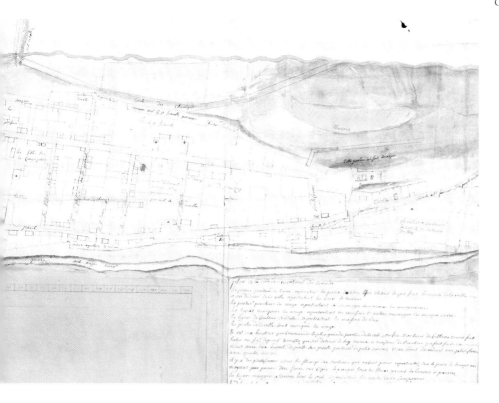

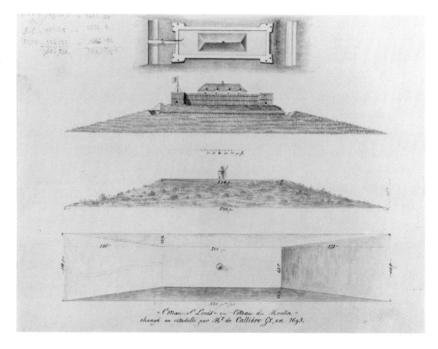

« Côteau St Louis » ou Côteau du Moulin » changé en citadelle par Mr de Callière Gr en. 1693.

hung the chapel, using bastions and canon rigs. These preparations took place in 1693, the same year that Testard de Montigny built his two-storey wooden house on *place* Bonsecours and the very same year, need it be added, that his military career took off. For Jacques Testard de Montigny was a man of some distinction. A friend of Pierre Le Moyne d'Iberville, he joined Le Moyne in military expeditions to New England, Newfoundland and Acadia. He became an able tactician familiar with the war methods of the natives that he used in his campaigns against the English posts. Although he was frequently away from Montreal, de Montigny nevertheless had a large family since his second wife, Marie de La Porte de Louvigny, bore him seven children. He died in Montreal in 1737 at the age of seventy-four. His Montreal house would remain in the family until the middle of the eighteenth century. Archaeologists recently found a section of the wall of this property in the present yard of Notre-Dame-de-Bon-

Secours Chapel, and it is probable that the remains of this impressive residence, reconstructed in stone in 1724, are partially intact under the asphalt surface.

As for neighbours, Testard de Montigny was certainly in good company. Two notable French Canadian families, Le Moyne de Longueuil and Pécaudy de Contrecoeur, influential both in the government of New France and in its commerce, were prosperous and highly-respected residents at the east end of *rue* Saint-Paul from the beginning of the eighteenth century, even before the palisade took in this part of the town. An important consideration for these prominent men was that, at the time, the Bonsecours district remained the only part of town in which it was still possible to build large houses. Charles Le Moyne, received into the nobility with the title of baron de Longueuil by Louis XIV in 1700, would occupy the post of major of Montreal in 1706, of governor of Montreal in 1724 and would be interim governor general of New France the following year. He built himself a house just west of the chapel in 1701. Perhaps he found it a good spot for making the crossing between Montreal and Longueuil on the south shore. Until his death in 1743, François-Antoine Pécaudy de Contrecoeur lived in the house next to Testard de Montigny. He and his wife, Jeanne de Saint-Ours, were descendants of captains of the Carignan-Salières regiment who arrived in Canada in 1665 and had been well-etablished members of the colony ever since. Two of their daughters married well. Marie-Françoise married Jean-Hugues Péan de Livaudière, commander of trading posts then major of Quebec; her sister Louise married François Daine, lieutenant-general of the military police in Quebec, a man well-regarded by Intendant François Bigot; Louise herself was a favourite of Bigot who will be considered later in relation to the *affaire du Canada*.

After military installations were constructed on the old mill hill, the palisade underwent the first changes to its layout in order to include the Jesuit property. At this time in the *faubourg* Bonsecours, the layout of the roads was gradually adapted to suit the location of gates cut into the enclosure of the town. *Rue* Saint-Paul, still unnamed

TRACES OF STAKES of the palisade found by the archaeologists near the apse of the stone chapel. The wooden fortifications of Montreal were extended twice to take in new parts of the growing town. This one, intended to protect the *faubourg* Bonsecours, dates from 1709 or 1710.

Photograph: Pierre Fauteux, Ville de Montréal

and unmapped once beyond the town limits, gradually came to be known under that name during the years 1690-1700.

But above all, it is the *chemin* Saint-François, designated as such from 1691, that is of interest. An almost completely forgotten vestige of the old town, cut off and renamed on numerous occasions — Saint Francis, Bonneau, Friponne — *rue* Saint-François is the key to understanding the positioning of the first stone chapel. Even today, the city grid shows traces of this primitive trail that led to the river from the chapel, branching onto *rue* Saint-Martin: *rue* Friponne.

ENTER THE MILITARY
The development of the *faubourg* took a decisive turn in 1709 when the royal authorities began a second extension of the palisade. This time, the chapel and the citadel hill became part of the enclosure, but the *faubourg* itself was cut in two. From the eastern wall of the chapel, the stockade cut across *rue* Saint-François, followed the top of the river embankment and climbed north along the property next to Monsieur de Montigny and in line with the present *rue* Bonneau. The

Saint-Martin gate on *rue* Saint-Paul — one of nineteen gates of the enclosure — permitted access to the town to the fifteen landowners excluded by the new plan.

The life of the old *faubourg*, now a district, changed again with the arrival of another social class, the military. In town, the garrison lodged with the local population throughout the French regime, which saved the government from building barracks. The authorities who had already taken over the hill reasserted their presence in the area. The king's warehouses were built in the district and the military character of Montreal became more evident in 1713 following the order of the intendant, Michel Bégon, requiring construction of stone fortifications. The huge work site opened in 1717 under the direction of the military engineer Gaspard-Joseph Chaussegros de Léry. The fortifications in the Bonsecours sector were completed in 1735 and a gate known as the underground gate, no doubt because of the steep slope, was cut through the high wall at the end of the lane beside the chapel leading to the river's edge.

The new enclosure pushed back the town limits once more, finally encompassing all the properties in the *faubourg*, including the huge area reserved for the royal canoe shed. The district craftsmen found this enforced proximity to their advantage. The shoemakers and the iron-workers in the area undoubtedly counted the Montreal garrison among their clients and the garrison was responsible for provisioning the forts in the backcountry. But the quiet development of industry and the unfolding of time in the Bonsecours district were suddenly disrupted by an event that took place outside the district in the heart of Montreal.

A FINAL RESTING PLACE

On 10 April 1734, for the third time in its history, the Hôtel-Dieu de Montréal was totally devastated by fire. After the first fire in 1695, the nuns had found refuge for several months with their neighbours, the sisters of the Congrégation de Notre-Dame. Although they again found a temporary home with the Congregation after a second fire in 1721, it was quickly discovered that there was not enough space for the two communities and the Hôtel-Dieu nuns moved with their patients to a section of the Hôpital Général situated at Pointe-à-Callière. After the fire of 1734, the nuns and their patients moved to the large stone two-storey house built by Jacques de Montigny in 1724 on the site of the previous wooden dwelling. This house was judged suitable for two reasons: it was the largest house in Montreal and its proximity to Notre-Dame-de-Bon-Secours Chapel made it possible for these cloistered religious to use the chapel as their conventual church. The Hôtel-Dieu nuns continued to rent the house from M. de Montigny for three years during the reconstruction of their institution.

However, their misfortunes were far from over. In November 1734, one of the royal vessels landing in Quebec carried a serious epidemic. Among those allowed to come upriver to Montreal because they were considered free of disease was a soldier who fell ill on the trip and was sent to the hospital in the Montigny house on his arrival in Montreal. Between 13 November and 30 November 1734, nine of the nuns died of the unidentified contagion and were buried beneath Notre-Dame-de-Bon-Secours Chapel. Although the community would have liked to remove their remains to the rebuilt Hôtel-Dieu, this was not permitted for fear of spreading the contagion. The remains of these nine nuns still lie beneath the chapel.

THE CHAPEL PERISHES IN FLAMES

Exactly twenty years later, the little chapel of Notre-Dame-de-Bon-Secours was itself totally consumed by fire. Surprisingly, despite ample archaeological evidence of the violence of the fire that destroyed the chapel in 1754, very little documentary evidence has so far been discovered. Though the exact day and, at times, the exact hour of other notable fires in Montreal have been recorded, we do not know even the month in which this fire occurred. The *Histoire de la Congrégation de Notre-Dame* makes no mention of the event until the question of preserving the site arises. The Sulpician Étienne Montgolfier, who was in Montreal at the time, says in his biography of Marguerite Bourgeoys that the chapel was reduced to ashes when

THE DAY AFTER THE FIRE that destroyed the chapel in 1754. As if by a miracle, the little statue of the Virgin is retrieved from the smoking ruins.

Illustration: Francis Back, Marguerite Bourgeoys Museum

THE ARCHAEOLOGICAL DIG UNCOVERED TRACES OF THE FIRE OF 1754 that destroyed the first chapel. A heap of various kinds of debris, stone stained with soot, charred wood, glass twisted by the heat, scorched nails and some shards of scorched ceramic, all found in the same layer inside the razed walls of the chapel.

Collection of the ministère de la Culture et des Communications du Québec
Photograph: Pierre Fauteux, Marguerite Bourgeoys Museum

a fire consumed part of the town in 1754. The fact that the recent archaeological excavations did not uncover any traces of the sacred vessels would suggest either that, as in the 1734 fire at the Hôtel-Dieu, they were saved from the conflagration or that their remains were removed later. In his comments about the earlier history of Montreal, Jacques Viger tells us that the statuette given by the Baron de Fancamp was removed next day from the smouldering ruins, intact in its reliquary — a preservation regarded as miraculous given the intensity of the fire.

Further calamities loomed on the horizon. That same year, open rivalry with England and with the British colonies began again. The war effort delayed any plan to re-build the chapel. Shortly after the outbreak of the Seven Years War in 1756, one by one the French fortresses began to fall: first, Louisbourg, then Quebec and finally, in 1760, Montreal. The ruins of the little chapel were still evident in the Bonsecours district when the British garrison took control of the town. If the chapel was ever to rise again, it would be under the British flag.

CHAPTER 3

THE REBIRTH OF NOTRE-DAME-DE-BON-SECOURS (1755-1847)

THE SHOCK WAVE of the conflict between France and England made itself felt with great violence in New France, sometimes even in the most hidden corners of daily life. The change of regime in Montreal was not accomplished without disruption even though the city did not undergo military assault as did Quebec. The struggles of the war and the financial chaos that was the legacy of the old regime had left a large part of the population deeply distressed. Now came the breaking up of the traditional commercial networks and the arrival of a new elite, of British descent and overwhelmingly Protestant. All of this was the harbinger of a slow adaptation to a new political and economic landscape.

In such a context, the reconstruction of Notre-Dame-de-Bon-Secours Chapel was not one of the foremost priorities of the clergy. The problems facing Montrealers at this time were so great that, however much the loss of the little chapel might be regretted, there could be no question of an immediate reconstruction. Ironically, it was the threat of losing the site altogether that galvanized the citizens of Montreal into raising their first church from its ashes.

A CHAPEL OR A BARRACKS?

The British soldiers who arrived in Montreal after the Conquest of 1760 were at first billeted in homes and buildings belonging to the

PORTRAIT OF M. MONTGOLFIER
Archives of the *Séminaire de Saint-Sulpice*, Montreal

local population, a somewhat delicate situation. On 2 January 1766, they were ordered to evacuate these dwellings and repair to makeshift barracks on Citadel Hill. Displeased with their new quarters which they considered unhealthy, the soldiers set them on fire and prevented the local population, who feared a conflagration that would engulf the city, from putting out the flames. As a result, the authorities were forced to build more spacious barracks for the garrison which that year counted 860 soldiers.[1] The chief engineer selected as the most suitable site for the project an area left vacant for a dozen years: the piece of land where lay the ruins of Notre-Dame-de-Bon-Secours Chapel. A request was made to the Sulpicians and the wardens of Notre-Dame Parish to buy the property in the name of the king. The events that followed were carefully recorded in the *Registre des délibérations de la fabrique de la paroisse de Ville-Marie*.

The Sulpicians and the wardens of the parish now found themselves faced with a diplomatic problem. Relations between the new British authorities and the Catholic Church could be delicate and complicated. Even sympathetic British officials had to consider the anti-Catholic sentiment easily aroused among others of their countrymen. On 27 July 1767, Étienne Mongolfier, superior of the Séminaire de Saint-Sulpice and titular parish priest, and Louis Jollivet, who performed the actual function of pastor, convoked the council of the wardens of Notre-Dame. They carefully considered the request for the Bonsecours property laid before them, then composed a letter of masterful tact to the British authorities.

Their letter stated that the parish had already formed the intention of rebuilding the chapel and that since some donors had already contributed funds for the project and others had made pledges, the parish could not possibly withdraw from the land. However, if the site were absolutely necessary to the king's service, they added, it would be sold to him for a fair price and the money used to buy another site suitable for the reconstruction of the chapel. All this, of course, was subject to the authority of the bishop without whose consent they could not alienate church property. For whatever reason, the British

1. Phyllis LAMBERT and Allan STEWART, dir., *Opening the gates of eighteenth-century Montreal*, Montreal: Canadian Centre for Architecture, 1992, p.40.

Étienne Montgolfier, S.S.

Étienne Montgolfier was born in 1712 in Vidalon, France, and joined the Sulpicians on his ordination to the priesthood in 1741. He arrived in Montreal in October 1751 and was named superior there in January 1759. As superior, he automatically became administrator of the Sulpician seigneuries at Montreal, titular parish priest of Montreal and vicar general of the bishop of Quebec for the district of Montreal. He could scarcely have assumed these responsibilities at a more difficult time: Quebec had just surrendered to the British and Montreal itself would surrender on 8 September 1760. Bishop Henri-Marie Dubreil de Pontbriand had taken refuge in the Sulpician seminary in Montreal after the capitulation of Quebec. After the death of the bishop in June 1760, M. Montgolfier was the choice of the Quebec Cathedral Chapter as his successor, though the appointment went to Jean-Olivier Briand, the candidate preferred by General James Murray, governor of Canada. Much of Étienne Montgolfier's effort in the following years was devoted to the struggle to preserve the Catholic Church in the colony. As superior of the seminary and titular parish priest of Montreal, he played a leading role in saving the Bonsecours land from becoming the site of British barracks and in bringing about the reconstruction of the chapel. As ecclesiastical superior and chaplain to the Congrégation de Notre-Dame, he wrote *La vie de la vénérable sœur Marguerite Bourgeois*. To do so, he made an effort to collect the writings of Marguerite Bourgeoys which had been scattered and was able to question sisters who had lived with others who had known Marguerite Bourgeoys at first hand. When this book appeared in 1818, it was the first work of biography published in Canada. Étienne Montgolfier died in Montreal on 27 August 1791.

LA VIE

DE LA

VENERABLE SŒUR

MARGUERITE BOURGEOIS,

DITE

DU SAINT SACREMENT,

Institutrice, Fondatrice, et Première Supérieure des Filles Séculières de la

CONGREGATION NOTRE-DAME,

ETABLIE A VILLE-MARIE,

DANS

L'ISLE DE MONTREAL, EN CANADA,

TIRÉE DE MEMOIRES CERTAINS, ET LA PLUPART ORIGINAUX.

A VILLE-MARIE:

CHEZ WM. GRAY, RUE ST. PAUL.
1818.

TITLE PAGE of the biography of Marguerite Bourgeoys written by Étienne de Montgolfier, and published in 1818.

authorities withdrew their proposal and the barracks were built further east in the *faubourg* Québec.

Several more years were to elapse before the chapel rose from its ruins. The delays can be attributed to the economic difficulties of the times and also to several devastating fires in Montreal, among them the destruction of the mother house of the Congrégation de Notre-Dame in Old Montreal on the night of 11 to 12 April 1768. But when, at last, events began to move, they moved quickly and they were shaped in such a way as to parallel very closely those that accompanied the building of the first stone chapel nearly a hundred years before.

OUT OF THE ASHES

At their meeting held in the Seminary on *rue* Notre-Dame immediately after vespers on Sunday, 16 June 1771, the priests, wardens and parishioners of Notre-Dame Parish resolved on the immediate reconstruction of Notre-Dame-de-Bon-Secours Chapel "urgently requested by the citizens of this town." Three merchants, Étienne Augé, Jacques Lemoine and Pierre Gamelin, all wardens or former wardens, were entrusted with the task of drawing up a plan with sufficient space for the chapel and an estimate of the necessary work and materials for rebuilding so as to give the closest possible idea of what the projected chapel would cost.

Messieurs Augé, Lemoine and Gamelin were expeditious in fulfilling their assignment and on the following Sunday, 23 June 1771, they presented their report to the assembly. The *Délibérations* makes no mention of the figures projected but does tell us that the decision was made to seek subscriptions for the new building: Lemoine and Gamelin were to canvass the "principal citizens and bourgeois" and also the "new subjects" of the town. The latter reference perhaps foreshadows the growing role the new chapel would play in the lives of English-speaking Montreal Catholics in the following century. The craftsmen, still numerous in the Bonsecours area, were to be approached by Charles Lefebvre and Joseph Papineau *dit* Montigny.

On Saturday, 29 June 1771, Étienne Montgolfier freely ceded the land for the chapel to the *fabrique* of the parish, the first formal recording of the cession of land for Notre-Dame-de-Bon-Secours Chapel. In the *Délibérations* this is described as "all the land belonging to the said gentlemen [the Sulpicians] lying between the house of Monsieur Deschambault and that of the late Monsieur Montigny where the house called *la friponne* now stands". Louis Jollivet then planted a cross on the site designated for the rebuilding of the chapel. The next day, after vespers at Notre-Dame Church, a solemn procession wended its way to the site. The dignitaries carried with them treasures from the first stone chapel: the foundation stone with the "lead plaque and the medal of the Blessed Virgin" that had been discovered on the site when the foundations for the new chapel were dug. These objects were once more laid in the foundations where they would remain until their accidental rediscovery in 1945.

So began the laying of the foundation stones of the church, an ancient ceremony whose symbolism is based on Ephesians 2: 20-22, "You are part of a building that has apostles and prophets for its foundations and Christ Jesus himself for its main cornerstone. As every structure is aligned on him, all grow into one holy temple in the Lord; and you too, in him, are being built into a house where God lives, in the Spirit."

The first of the new foundation stones was laid by M. Montgolfier. Then ten other dignitaries, including some of the most prominent citizens of the time, placed stones at various locations along the walls. The names of these ten men, as recorded in the *Délibérations,* were Roch St-Ours de Deschaillons, Luc DeChapt de la Corne, François-Marie Picoté de Belestre, Joseph Dominique Emmanuel Le Moyne de Longueuil, Ignace Bourassa la Ronde, Pierre Gamelin, Jacques Porlier, Jacques Lemoine, Étienne Augé, Thomas Dufy Desaunais. Finally, below the threshold of the centre door, Louis Jollivet laid with the last foundation stone a plaque with a Latin inscription that translates:

FOUNDATION STONE AND LEAD PLAQUE OF THE 1771-1775 CHAPEL. While an opening was being made in the basement of the chapel for a door on to *rue* de la Commune in 1945, the chaplain discovered one of the foundation stones of the second chapel, as well as the commemorative plaques of both chapels.

Photographs: Pierre Fauteux, Ville de Montréal (above)
Marguerite Bourgeoys Museum (below)

> This temple, dedicated to God, great and good, and to the blessed Mary Auxiliatrix under the title of her Assumption; built first in 1675 on smaller dimensions, then consumed by flames in 1754, has been re-established and enlarged by the citizens of Ville-Marie … on 30 June 1771, the same day on which the first stone of the old church was laid.

Just as the bronze engraving of the Blessed Virgin had been placed with the first foundation stone in 1675, a silver medal of Pope Clement XIII having on its reverse side an image of Charity with a horn of plenty and the words *Dedit Pauperibus*, that is, "he gave to the poor", was placed with this last stone. The stone laid by M. Montgolfier was discovered in 1945 but the others must still lie beneath the walls of the present chapel. Each of the stones placed by the ten dignitaries bore a lead plaque detailing the name and qualities of the man who laid it there.

Within a month, however, it seemed that other circumstances from the past might repeat themselves. Marguerite Bourgeoys' first attempt to build the chapel was delayed in 1657 when the Jesuits were replaced by the Sulpicians in Montreal. Now it seemed that a change in the British colonial administration might have the same effect on the second chapel. At their meeting of 28 July 1771, the wardens of the parish were informed of the reception of a letter from Hector Cramahé. Cramahé had become administrator of the province the previous August during the absence in England of the governor, Sir Guy Carleton, and in June 1771, had been appointed lieutenant governor of the colony. From the wardens' response to this letter, some of its contents can be deduced. It is apparent that someone had made a complaint against the rebuilding of the chapel alleging that it blocked the public street and would be a detriment to the public good. Worse still, Cramahé accused the wardens of proceeding without authorization. Their reply to Cramahé begins:

> The letter you were pleased to write to Monsieur Montgolfier on the 20th of this month has been communicated to us in our assembly today; we are grieved to see that your honour appears antagonized against us on the subject of the rebuilding and enlarging of our burned chapel. We never thought, in undertaking this building, that it would draw the attention of your honour to our work or we would not have hesitated to inform you and we believe that when you know why we began you will not disapprove of our manner of acting on this occasion.

The explanations that follow tell us much of the role the first chapel had come to play in the Bonsecours area and the *faubourg* Québec. They imply that, even before it was destroyed by fire, the chapel had begun to serve as an annex to the parish church. The citizens of the district, the letter claims, had for some time urgently demanded the reconstruction of the chapel and sorrowed to find themselves "deprived of the Mass which was said for them each day in this place that is close by and was always the great devotion of the town." The reconstruction is, then, a good opportunity to enlarge the chapel because the parish church has become too small for the crowds on most feast days of the year. When the first chapel was built, there were fewer than fifty baptisms a year in the parish while now there are four hundred, a good indication of the growth of the Montreal population.

The letter goes on to deny that the new building is encroaching on *rue* Saint-Paul as Cramahé had been informed. The wardens stress the damaging effect of interrupting the construction, already underway, of a large stone vault which, far from being a detriment to the public, would be a protection against fire in the area. Finally, they point out that the new chapel will, in fact, enhance the district.

Happily, the construction of the second chapel was not delayed. The incident closed with another letter from the lieutenant governor granting permission for the rebuilding and extension of the chapel. While this letter contained an assurance that no worry or embarrassment had been intended, it also insisted on the "Deference" and "Submission" owed to the king. On 30 June 1773, the new chapel was blessed though the interior decoration was not yet complete. The mason was Joseph Morin and the carpenter, Pierre Raza *dit* Rangeard but the name of the architect is unknown. The building was simple and remained faithful in spirit to the old regime with its double-lanterned bell tower, its windows with rounded arches and its circular window in the gable. It measured 70 by 46 feet (21.3 by 14 metres), with a many-sided sanctuary 32 by 30 feet (9.7 by 9.1 metres) erected over a half-domed vault.

It was a source of grief to the sisters of the Congrégation de Notre-Dame that they were unable at this time to contribute to the building of the new chapel on the same scale as they had done for the first. The loss of their mother house in the fire of 1768 and the expense of rebuilding it had placed considerable strain on their financial resources. However, remembering, perhaps, how Marguerite Bourgeoys had taken in sewing to reimburse the first settlers for their work on the chapel in 1657, they found another way of contributing to the building fund:

> The Community supplied for Bon-Secours the value of one year of laundry for the parish church, which comes to a little more than 600 *livres*. We gilded the little niche of the Blessed Virgin on the tabernacle of Bon-Secours. We also made the candles and did the laundry for the same church for a year, gratis.[2]

In fact, it would seem that after its reconstruction there was not a great deal of money available from any source to spend on the upkeep and decoration of the chapel. In his history of Notre-Dame-de-Bon-Secours Chapel published in 1900, Jean-Marie Leleu compares it to a poor little girl forced to dress in her grandmother's outmoded dresses. He was thinking, no doubt, of an organ case received from the parish church in 1795, and in 1830, at the time of the construction of the new Notre-Dame Church, of a baldaquin of the school of Quévillon. Records also show sums expended for repairs to the spire, the bell tower, the front entrance and the roof where, in 1815, shingles were replaced by tin plate. In 1823, the sculptor Louis-Xavier Leprohon was commissioned to repair and paint the wooden vault of the chapel.

STONE CROSS FROM THE PEDIMENT OF THE CHAPEL. Seen in its original location in this photograph taken in 1884, *rue* Saint-Paul. When a new façade was attached to the old one at the end of the nineteenth century, the cross was stored in the basement of the chapel where the archaeologists found it in 1997.

Old photograph: National Archives of Canada, C65381 (detail)
Recent photograph: Pierre Fauteux, Ville de Montréal

2. *Histoire de la Congrégation de Notre-Dame*, V, p.194. Trans.

The Rebirth of Notre-Dame-de-Bon-Secours ✤ 71

Baldaquin, altar and holy water font

The baldaquin from the old Notre-Dame Church had a place of honour in the sanctuary of Notre-Dame-de-Bon-Secours chapel. Some time before its installation, an inventory of the chapel was included in an inventory of Notre-Dame parish completed by Jean Guillaume Delisle in 1792. In it we learn, among other things, that the chapel contained three wooden altars and three wooden tabernacles, painted and gilded. One of these tabernacles was surmounted by the gilded niche containing the little statue of Notre-Dame de Bon-Secours. Besides the usual altar vessels and books, hangings, linens and chandeliers, there were a number of pictures, several of subjects traditionally associated with the chapel: the Assumption of the Virgin, Saint Anne, Saint Joseph. There is mention of twenty large benches in the nave, of a large holy water font in cut stone and of a small one in copper.

THE BALDAQUIN OF THE PARISH CHURCH AND ORIGINAL DOORS OF THE SECOND CHAPEL. After the demolition of the first parish church, the baldaquin designed by Louis Quévillon, Joseph Pépin and Paul Rollin in 1808 was moved to Notre-Dame-de-Bon-Secours. The photograph also shows the original doors in the chapel (1773).

Detail of a photograph taken in 1884. Notman Photographic Archives, McCord Museum of Canadian History, Montreal, view 1320

DECORATIVE MOULDINGS ATTRIBUTED TO THE SCULPTOR LEPROHON. These gilded wood and plaster mouldings were found in the cellar of the chapel during the archaeological dig in 1997. They are probably part of the vault decorated by Leprohon in 1823.

Photographs: Pierre Fauteux, Marguerite Bourgeoys Museum

The Sailors' Chapel

The changes in Notre-Dame-de-Bon-Secours Chapel reflected the changes taking place in Montreal at the end of the eighteenth century. Until then, Montreal had been largely a post for the fur trade. In the last quarter of the eighteenth century, the city began its transformation into the great port it would become in the nineteenth century. The *Manuel du Pèlerin,* published in 1848, furnishes this information:

> In 1784-85, the church wardens erected the large building next to the church of which the third floor, on the same level as the sanctuary, forms the sacristy. On the side of this building that faces the river, one can still see a recess made in one of the piers where devotion to the Blessed Virgin had caused to be placed a picture that the ravages of time have destroyed. This image invited the many sailors who sail our great river to invoke with confidence, in the midst of their distant journeys and continual dangers, Her whom the Church calls and who is, for so many reasons, the Star of the Sea.

NOTRE-DAME-DE-BON-SECOURS DRAWN BY FÉLIX MARTIN, S.J., around 1844. At the time, the bishop was planning to give the chapel to the Jesuits, a decision that was never carried out. It is possible to make out the corner of the Masonic Hall (British American Hotel) just a few years before the construction of Bonsecours Market.

Watercolour, Félix Martin, S.J., around 1844-1846
Jesuit archives, Saint-Jérôme, Québec, BO-47-1,17

LA FRIPONNE (THE CHEAT)

While the foundations of the new Notre-Dame-de-Bon-Secours Chapel were being laid in Montreal, in Paris a certain Louis Pennisseaut was just having his name cleared, exempting him from a heavy fine and from banishment for life from the French capital. Arrested for fraud in 1761 and imprisoned in the Bastille for the *affaire du Canada* with François Bigot, the intendant of New France, this Pennisseaut is none other than the owner of the big warehouse that Montrealers had derisively named "*la Friponne*" — "the Cheat".

The interest of Bigot and his associates in the *Bonsecours* district went back several years. Ever since 1749, on each of his stop-overs in Montreal, François Bigot stayed at the "*Intendance*", a large building located on the old property of Charles Le Moyne where, a century later, Bonsecours Market would be built. In the first years of the Seven Years War, the growth of the private company owned by Bigot and his associates required the building of warehouses in Quebec and in Montreal. One of the fronts in these commercial transactions was Louis Pennisseaut. It was he who bought the land next to Notre-

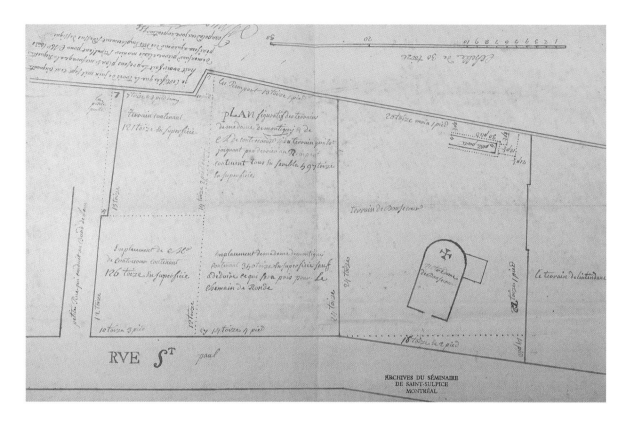

The following labels appear on the plan: *Plan figuratif des terrains demandez par madame de Montigny et de Mr de Conttrecoeur*, *Terrain de Bonsecour*, *Notre Dame de Bonsecours*, *RVE ST paul*

IN 1758, FOUR YEARS AFTER THE FIRE THAT DESTROYED NOTRE-DAME-DE-BON-SECOURS CHAPEL and the De Montigny house, the vacant lots attracted the interest of speculators. Louis Pennisseaut purchased the De Montigny site to build the warehouse called *la Friponne*.

Archives of the *Séminaire de Saint-Sulpice*, Montreal
Photograph: Christian Poulin, Marguerite Bourgeoys Museum

Dame-de-Bon-Secours Chapel from the de Montigny heirs in 1758. The property included the ruins of the house of the late Testard de Montigny that burned down in the same fire that destroyed the chapel.

The following year, Pennisseaut built a two-storey warehouse on the spot which housed a bakery and a butcher shop. Then he sold the property to Joseph Cadet, a munitions supplier and one of the ablest of Bigot's confederates. The use of the building for shops is far from insignificant. Cadet and Pennisseaut were in business with Bigot to provide supplies to the troops and the forts of the back country. Cadet was responsible for supplying bread, meat and peas to the soldiers on campaign and in the town garrisons. It isn't difficult to imagine the importance of *la Friponne* warehouse in this flourishing business with the government. The immense profits made by Bigot and his henchmen turned this story into a scandal at a time when the population of New France was suffering from the inflation and scarcity of goods brought on by the Seven Years War: some staple foods cost up to seven times as much as in Paris. Imprisoned in the Bastille in 1761, most of the men who were suspects in what came to be called the *affaire du Canada* went to trial two years later. Convictions for embezzlement and corruption carried fairly stiff fines and, for a number of these men, François Bigot among them, would entail lifetime banishment from France, while Pennisseaut was exiled from Paris for nine years. Many, however, would see their penalties reduced and their cases reviewed a few years later.

Like the rest of Montreal, the Bonsecours area began to change after the Conquest. The re-building of the chapel seemed to attract the interest of the merchants to a district that until then had been the exclusive domain of craftsmen and the military. The impact of the long years of war on the lives of Montrealers gradually lessened; activities of everyday life were resumed but based now on new economic partnerships. Pierre Gamelin, one of the wardens of Notre-Dame who played an important role in the reconstruction of the chapel, had his own reasons for promoting the development of the district. In 1760, he had acquired a large property to the west of the chapel; then, between 1772 and 1778, he became co-owner of *la Friponne* with Pierre du Calvet and Jacques Lemoine.

In 1789, the *fabrique* of Notre-Dame acquired the land and the building known as *la Friponne*, measuring 120 feet by 30 feet (40 by 9 metres) according to the deed of sale. For several years, the *fabrique* leased the premises of the warehouse-bakery to William Logan, master baker, then, in 1815, to another baker, Thomas Rainier.

THE *quartier* BONSECOURS AT THE
BEGINNING OF THE NINETEENTH
CENTURY. Citadel Hill still
dominates the landscape, Notre-
Dame-de-Bon-Secours holds the
place of honour and John
Molson's Mansion House is right
next to the chapel. All that is left
of the fortifications are bits and
pieces, including the Quebec Gate
that remains intact to the extreme
east.

Watercolour attributed to William
Berczy. Album Jacques Viger,
Ville de Montréal, gestion de
documents et archives

THE FORTIFICATIONS DISAPPEAR ... AND SO DOES THE HILL!

The city was the setting for spectacular changes in the first decades of
the nineteenth century. At least three projects had an immediate impact
on the residents of the Bonsecours district and on the property ownership of the *fabrique*: the demolition of the fortifications, the laying out
of Montreal's first aqueduct and the levelling of Citadel Hill.

The citizens of Montreal had been calling for the demolition of
the stone enclosure for years when in 1801 the authorities finally
passed a law providing for the razing of fortifications which had
become dilapidated. The work took fifteen years to complete and
made way for a new era of town planning. In fact, drainage projects
were already well underway and someone who would soon become
famous in Montreal actively contributed to the urban reforms.
Jacques Viger, son of Jacques Viger the shoemaker whose family
had lived in the Bonsecours district for several generations, was
closely involved in these projects. Thanks to his family connections —

Jacques Viger

A figure inseparable from the *quartier* Bonsecours, Jacques Viger was the husband of Marie-Marguerite La Corne with whom he had three children who did not survive childhood. He was the first mayor of Montreal and the designer of its coat of arms and of its motto. One of his relatives, Amédée Papineau, provides a very colourful portrait of the man:

For my father and mother, Jacques Viger was "the neighbour". And not a day went by that he didn't arrive around nine or ten o'clock in the evening to share with them the news and gossip of the day … He was the ugliest, most eccentric, kindest and most cheerful man I have ever known. He was both an antiquarian and a book lover, always rooting around in the court archives, parish, seigneury, seminary and convent registers; often sketching on site the ruins of the old forts, churches, mills and ramparts that were to be found throughout the length and breadth of the country. A poet and a singer, he would arrive at a dinner party, either private or public, with both new and old songs because people still sang in those days. Then he would record all of it in *Ma Saberdache*, manuscript volumes close to one hundred in number which Father Verreau, director of the École normale de Montréal, inherited and which he was to have printed for posterity.[3]

PORTRAIT OF JACQUES VIGER, ATTRIBUTED TO JAMES DUNCAN

Musée de la civilisation, collection of the *Séminaire du Québec*, no. 1993-15152

he was a cousin of Louis-Joseph Papineau and of Bishop Jean-Jacques Lartigue — Viger had great influence in the city administration. For several years beginning in 1813, Viger was inspector of the main roads, streets, lanes and bridges of Montreal. He reported on the sanitary conditions of the districts, the drainage system along the streets and the layout of public squares. Throughout this period, his family and the Papineau family continued to be among the principal landowners of the district.

3. Amédée PAPINEAU, *Souvenirs de jeunesse 1822-1837*, Sillery, Québec, Cahiers du Septentrion, 1998, 42-43. Trans.

In 1805, the *fabrique* used the opportunity offered by the demolition of the fortifications to acquire the stretch of road along Water Street — now *rue* de la Commune — in a transaction registered with the notary Chaboillez. Thus, the *fabrique* became proprietor of all the lots in the area surrounding the chapel, an area that became known as the "terrain Bonsecours" (the Bonsecours land). Part of the vacant land was rented out as a wood yard.

Because of their proximity to the river and to Citadel Hill, new aqueduct installations would also be located in the Bonsecours district. Thomas Porteous, director of the Water Works Company since 1816, planned to provide Montrealers with potable water

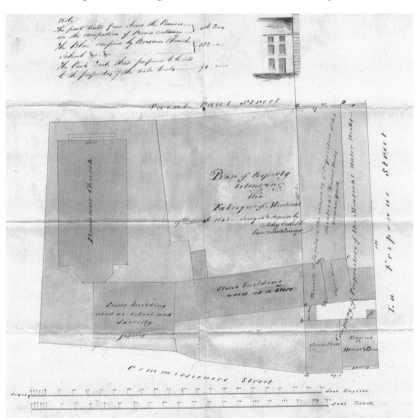

PLAN DRAWN BY JOHN OSTELL. This plan shows a parcel of the Bonsecours land purchased by the Montreal Water Works Company in 1842.

Archives of the Marguerite Bourgeoys Museum

through the latest technology developed in Scotland: a steam pump that would draw water from the river into the reservoir situated on the hill. The pumping station, joined by the town's first public baths and a flour mill, stood close to the warehouse, *la Friponne*, on Water Street. A few years later, Moses Judah Hayes, the new proprietor of the Water Works Company, exchanged a piece of land with the *fabrique* to become owner of the site where the main cast iron water pipes were laid.

The reservoir to allow the distribution of water to customers by gravity, originally meant to be installed on Citadel Hill, was instead laid out along the new section of *rue* Notre-Dame. Indeed, the government had decided to level the hill to permit the extension of *rue* Notre-Dame to the east so that, in 1819, the hill disappeared forever from the Montreal landscape. The Crown awarded the contract to level the hill to the merchants Oliver Wait and Stanley Bagg, who themselves hired a sub-contractor, the American Jedediah Hubbell Dorwin. In his personal journal, the latter recounts the details of this major event in the history of Montreal:

> This spring, [1819] in May, I made a contract with Bagg and Wait to level the Citadel Hill, they having been employed by the Government. This was rather a large job for me to undertake. I had the north half which was fifty five feet high. The earth to be removed toward St. Lewis Street to fill up the pond of water there, which, some people say, was dug out to make the hill and done by the French the first Settlers of the country. But which I found was not the case, for we found as the work advanced, the different kinds of soil would not warrant that supposition. There being layers of sea sand and then gravel the whole way up to the top of the hill. This year there was a large emigration mostly from Ireland so that I had no difficulty getting all [the] labourers that I could place on the work, so by the fall I had the job completed which was only a moderate paying contract. Bagg and Wait carried on the other half themselves.[4]

After the demolition of the fortifications and the levelling of Citadel Hill, the military continued to maintain a presence in the Bonsecours area. The Act of 1801 stated, in fact, that the Crown main-

4. Jedediah HUBBELL DORWIN, "Diaries", I, 75-76, NAC, MG 24, D12.

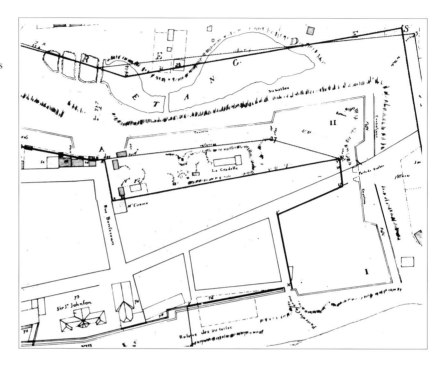

tained ownership of the Citadel, the Champ-de-Mars and the neigh-bouring barracks in the *faubourg* Québec. The soldiers concentrated their activities around the new fort built on *Île* Ste-Hélène in the 1820s but continued to occupy and develop their facilities in the *faubourg* Québec.

A LARGER CHAPEL FOR A GROWING POPULATION

The face of the district changed in keeping with the changes taking place in Montreal. If many craftsmen still lived in the Bonsecours area throughout the second half of the eighteenth century, they became less and less numerous in the first decades of the nineteenth. The property occupied by the Brazeau family from 1690 to 1743, at the corner of Saint-Paul and Bonsecours streets, was bought by Pierre du Calvet in 1770. Other families, like the Vigers and the Papineaus, rose in social status. Jacques Viger, the son of a shoemaker, became an administrator, a historian and a man of culture. Louis-Joseph Papineau's crafts-man grandfather had lived in a house on *rue* Bonsecours: his father, a notary, bought the property in 1809. Many of the British also be-came landowners in the area. A certain John Gray, merchant, acquired plots of land in the area lying east of the chapel.

In this rapidly changing society, it is apparent that Notre-Dame-de-Bon-Secours Chapel was no longer a place of pilgrimage, a fact deplored by Bishop Ignace Bourget in 1847. It is unclear when the practice of pilgrimage to the chapel fell into disuse. Did it coincide with the inclusion of the chapel within the city walls in 1709 or with its increasing use as an annex to the parish church? As we have seen in the deliberations preceding the reconstruction of 1771, the chapel, even before the Conquest, had been used to relieve crowding in Notre-Dame Church. There is no mention of pilgrimage in the discus-sions preceding the rebuilding of the chapel: the urgent reason behind its reconstruction was the increasing incapacity of the old parish church to accommodate the growing Montreal population especially on Sundays and feast days. As early as 1789, the wardens of Notre-Dame parish had been advised by the bishop to economize in view of saving toward the construction of a new parish church. In the next decades the problem was to become more and more acute as, in the nineteenth century, the population of Montreal began to increase at a rate of 3% a year, going from 9,000 to 57,715 between 1800 and 1852.

Two attempts were made by the wardens of Notre-Dame Parish to have Notre-Dame-de-Bon-Secours Chapel erected into a parish, the first in 1804, the second in 1816. Both were refused by Bishop Jo-seph-Octave Plessis. Instead, it was suggested that the capacity of the chapel be increased by the same method used in the parish church: the addition of two galleries to provide an additional 450 places. For French-speaking Catholics, the situation was eased by the construc-tion of Montreal's first cathedral, inaugurated in 1825, and of the new Notre-Dame Church, now Notre-Dame Basilica, blessed on the feast of Pentecost, 7 June 1829. By that time, however, the chapel was

RUE BONSECOURS, 1841. This is the façade of the chapel from the original construction of 1771 with its double-lanterned bell tower. *Rue* Bonsecours resembles the present-day street in many ways.

Watercolour by Philip John Bainbrigge. National Archives of Canada, C-011908

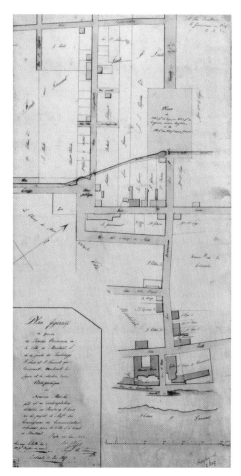

THE CHAPEL AND THE SURROUND-
ING DISTRICT IN 1817. Among
the residents were Jacques Viger,
Louis-Joseph Papineau and
Toussaint Pothier as well as the
Widow Fraser and a certain
Wragg.

Plan by Jacques Viger, 1817. National
Archives of Canada, NMC-1505

serving yet another need of a changing Montreal: it had become the cradle of the English-speaking Catholic community.

If the name of Jacques Viger heads the list of bench holders in the chapel in 1821 alongside such personages as the Baronne de Longueuil and Victoire Papineau and other famous names from the French regime, the names "Veuve Fraser", "Docteur Selby", Smith, Taylor, McDonald and Doyle also appear. In all, there are at least fourteen English, Irish and Scottish names out of a total of seventy-four, and two pews are set aside for the use of the Catholic officers of the garrison. One of the most important persons associated with the use of the chapel by English-speaking Catholics in the first decades of the nineteenth century was Jackson John Richards.

Jackson John Richards was born in Virginia in 1787 and became an itinerant Methodist minister. He arrived in Montreal by boat in August 1807 with the intention, apparently, of converting the Sulpicians to Protestantism. Instead, he became a Catholic, continued his theological studies in Mont-real, was ordained a priest in Notre-Dame Church in July 1813 and was admitted to the Sulpi-cians in February 1817. From 1815 to 1820, he served Notre-Dame-de-Bon-Secours Chapel where he gathered together the English-speaking Catholics of Montreal, many of them of Irish origin. In 1831, he was officially made the priest responsible for English-speaking Catholics who, by then, were assembling in the chapel of the Recollet monastery in the north-west corner of Old Montreal because their numbers had overflowed Notre-Dame-de-

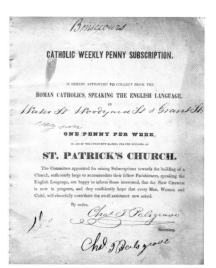

FRONTISPIECE OF THE SUBSCRIPTION
BOOK for the construction of Saint
Patrick's Church.

Marguerite Bourgeoys Museum

Bon-Secours Chapel. However, until 1846, Irish names continue to appear among those of the priests serving the chapel: the Sulpicians, Michael O'Brien, Patrick Morgan and James McMahon and the secular priest, Peter O'Connell. A small notebook in the archives of the Marguerite Bourgeoys Museum records the collections taken up each Sunday from July 1843 to July 1844 to assist in the building of a Church, "sufficiently large to accommodate the fellow Parishioners, speaking the English Language." That church, Saint Patrick's, was completed in 1847; until 1955 the Sulpicians continued to serve that parish and its parishioners, to make a yearly pilgrimage to Notre-Dame-de-Bon-Secours Chapel where their community had had its beginnings. This practice continued at least a decade after the Sulpicians were replaced by secular priests.

THE LITTLE SCHOOL

There was still another way in which the chapel came to be associated with the English-speaking Catholics of Montreal in the 1830s. Initially, it was one more consequence of the military presence in the area. Among the troops sent from England to suppress the rebellions of 1837-38 were several Catholic families who found themselves forced to send their children to the Protestant school in the barracks. When this was brought to the attention of Joseph-Vincent Quiblier, Superior of Saint-Sulpice, he arranged for classes to be set up in the building that had been constructed adjacent to the chapel in 1784-85. There is some evidence that private classes had sometimes been conducted in this building by lay teachers. The new classes occupied rooms below the sacristy that was located on the third floor. M. Quiblier requested of the Superior of the Congrégation de Notre-Dame two sisters able to teach in English. On 21 November 1838, Sister Saint-François-Xavier (Mary O'Donoughue), of Irish descent, and Sister Sainte-Ursule (Mary Ann Gibson), of Scottish descent, opened Bonsecours School. This school functioned until the departure of the regiment in 1846. For the following three years, a lay teacher conducted classes there for the boys of the area. In 1849, the sisters

Mary Ann Gibson (Sister Sainte-Ursule)

Mary Anne Gibson (Sister Sainte-Ursule) was, with Mary O'Donoughue (Sister Saint-François-Xavier), teacher of the two English classes opened below the sacristy of Notre-Dame-de-Bon-Secours Chapel in 1838. She was born in Quebec Lower Town, the second of three daughters in a Protestant family of Scottish origin. In 1897, less than six weeks before her death, she wrote: "Eighty-four years ago, I was a boarder at the convent in the Quebec Lower Town with my older sister when we were called to our mother's deathbed. Sister Saint-Henri, the superior of the convent, accompanied us. My mother, though Protestant, had a great respect for the sisters. The one who visited her was, for her, heaven sent. With complete confidence she told her: "I want to confide my little girls to you, to raise them and to teach them, so that they become angels like you." Then she said to my father: "It is my last wish." He hesitated; however, he consented and took us to the convent. The youngest was scarcely three years old. Shortly afterward, he died and we were orphans."

SISTER SAINTE-URSULE, BORN MARY ANN GIBSON. This photograph was taken many years after her posting as a teacher at the Bonsecours School.

Archives of the Congrégation de Notre-Dame de Montréal

The three girls were raised in the Congregation convent and became Catholics. The oldest and youngest became religious at the Hôtel-Dieu in Quebec and Mary Ann entered the Congrégation de Notre-Dame in Montreal in 1825. In 1864, she became the twenty-first superior of the Congrégation de Notre-Dame and the first to hold the title of Superior-General.

The first member of the Congrégation de Notre-Dame to celebrate seventy years of religious profession, she presided over great changes, not only in the form of government in the Congregation but in educational methods as well, and saw the establishment of fifteen new missions of the Congregation from Kankakee, Illinois, in the West to Tignish, Prince Edward Island, in the East. To the end of her life she took pride in the fact that her earliest days in the Congrégation de Notre-Dame had been spent with "venerable elderly sisters, among them Sister Saint-Ursule [Catherine Sabourin, whose religious name was given to Mary Anne Gibson on the death of the former], then aged eighty-five, who had spent her first years with the companions of our Venerable Mother Foundress, those who signed our first rules."

returned to open two French classes and one English class. Eventually the school came to serve only the French-speaking children of the area; it continued to receive an average of about 163 children a year until the demolition of the old building and the construction of a new building attached to the chapel in 1893. This building housed the school until its closure in 1968 and, in 1998, became part of the remodelled Marguerite Bourgeoys Museum.

NEW CONTEXT, NEW CHALLENGES

The changes taking place in the city extended to every aspect of society as is evident in the opening of the Theatre Royal on *rue* Saint-Paul, a few steps from the chapel. The project seems daring for the period since the Catholic clergy generally disapproved of such secular pursuits, but the promoters were beyond the influence of the clergy. Several members of the business community, among whom John Molson was a major shareholder, subscribed to the construction of this first building devoted to theatre arts in Montreal.

The Theatre Royal opened in 1825; Charles Dickens, the novelist, who was part of a British troupe, performed there in 1842. The following year, a French opera troupe performed. But two years later, the theatre was closed to make way for Bonsecours Market.

Another building, the Masonic Hall Hotel, important both for its size and for its architectural style, appeared between the chapel and the Theatre Royal. This site, long occupied by the Intendance built by Bigot, was bought by Joseph Fleury-Deschambault in 1760, then by John Johnson and finally by John Molson who had the building demolished in order to erect the Mansion House, a luxury hotel.

THE BRITISH AMERICAN HOTEL NEXT TO THE CHAPEL, *RUE SAINT-PAUL*. Known originally as the Masonic Hall, this hotel was erected in 1821 on the ruins of the Mansion House (1815), both properties of the Molson family. To the right of the hotel, the Theatre Royal.

Print taken from E.Z. Massicotte, *Cahier des Dix*, 1941

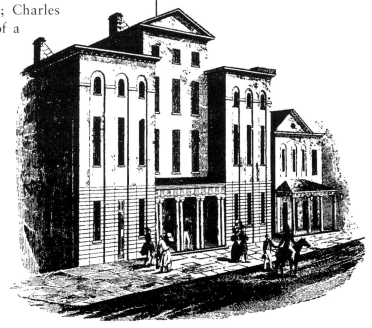

The little statue lost … and found

In 1831, the little statue of the madonna, with its reliquary, given to Marguerite Bourgeoys by the baron de Fancamp was spirited away from its place of honour over the tabernacle. It would not return permanently to the chapel for more than one hundred and fifty years.

The circumstances surrounding the loss, and, still more, the recovery of the statuette are extremely puzzling. The mystery that surrounds them may never be solved. The disappearance of the statue was attributed to theft by "a sacrilegious hand", made possible by the fact that the chapel was often deserted on weekdays outside the hours of Mass. In 1847, Bishop Ignace Bourget described it as a sign of the decrease in religious fervour.

In 1844, during the demolition of part of the mother house of the Congrégation de Notre-Dame in Old Montreal, the little statue was discovered, wrapped in waste paper and without its reliquary, in one of the attics. This statuette was kept carefully in the room of the Superior of the Congregation and not authenticated until the 1890s, so that, for most of the nineteenth century, the original statue of Notre-Dame-de-Bon-Secours remained officially missing. This careful conservation by successive superiors and the fact that only thirteen years elapsed between the disappearance of the little statue and its recovery cast doubt on the theory sometimes advanced that the statuette was not recognized. Was it concluded within the Congrégation de Notre-Dame that the statuette could be more easily safeguarded at the mother house? Certainly, its recovery does not seem to have been made known even to the bishop.

In 1894, during the restoration of the chapel, a dusty and neglected reliquary was found in the sacristy. When this was taken to the mother house of the Congrégation de Notre-Dame, it was found that the statuette recovered in 1844 fitted perfectly within it. Statue and niche were then identified as those given to Marguerite Bourgeoys by the Baron Pierre de Fancamp. At the instance of M. Henri Legrand, S.S., then chaplain at Notre-Dame-de-Bon-Secours, the statuette was returned to the chapel in 1935. From 1942, however, the statuette was once more at the mother house of the Congregation where, after the beatification of Marguerite Bourgeoys in 1950, it was venerated close to her tomb. On occasion, it was lent to the chapel.

On 17 April 1988, the statue made its formal and permanent return to Notre-Dame-de-Bon-Secours Chapel where it can be seen on the left side-altar behind a protective glass intended to preserve it from fire, theft and other dangers.

When this burned in 1821, Molson had it rebuilt as the Masonic Hall Hotel which later became the British American Hotel. Though this too suffered a fire in 1833, the building still seems to have been standing when John Molson Jr. sold the land to the city in 1844, as is evident in prints from the period. From then on, the presence of Bonsecours Market would be the beacon of a new era in the district and in the whole city: an era of commercial and industrial expansion.

In 1847, the future of the chapel that had risen from its ashes three quarters of a century before looked more uncertain than ever. The building of the new Notre-Dame Church, Saint Patrick's and the cathedral meant that it was no longer necessary to relieve crowding in Notre-Dame parish. Another unfortunate, some said ominous, event, had occurred in 1831. During the winter of that year, the oldest treasure of the chapel, the statuette of the Virgin given to Marguerite Bourgeoys in 1672, rescued from the ruins of the fire in 1754 and re-installed over the altar of the chapel in 1773, had been stolen, along with the reliquary studded with precious stones in which it was placed. When investigation failed to reveal the perpetrators of this theft or to find any trace of the statue, it was replaced with a large contemporary statue of Notre-Dame-de-la-Garde. Deprived of this link with its foundation and of the pastoral purposes it had come to serve, standing on land coveted by those whose over-riding concern was the commercial expansion and development of Montreal, would Notre-Dame-de-Bon-Secours Chapel, like so many other reminders of that first Ville-Marie, disappear before the rising tide of commerce, industry and "progress"?

CHAPTER 4

THE CHAPEL IN THE MARKETPLACE (1848-1882)

Surprisingly, perhaps, in an era when the idea of material progress seemed to reign supreme in Montreal, Notre-Dame-de-Bon-Secours Chapel was to survive the nineteenth century through a return to the spiritual purpose for which Marguerite Bourgeoys had established it in the first place: it would become once more a chapel of pilgrimage. But the event that led to this renewal was truly horrific, the typhus epidemic carried to Montreal by the Irish immigrants in 1847.

MONTREAL FACES ANOTHER DEADLY EPIDEMIC

To read about the circumstances of the Irish immigration to Canada in the first half of the nineteenth century is to enter a world of appalling suffering and anguish. Desperate to escape misery and starvation in their homeland, Irish men, women and children became a human cargo on ships returning from the transportation of potash and timber from Canada to England. These passengers were often in a weakened state before they boarded ships where they were packed like animals in unsanitary conditions that frequently led to outbreaks of cholera and typhoid fever. Despite attempts at quarantine, these diseases infected not only the Irish immigrants but also the local population with whom they came into contact when they landed. This was not the first major epidemic in nineteenth-century Montreal. In 1832 and 1834, Asiatic cholera had afflicted several thousand victims, striking immigrants and local citizens alike. In 1847, the scourge carried to the city was typhus.

Illustration page 88: The chapel in winter in the 19th century.

Unknown artist; Archives of the Marguerite Bourgeoys Museum

REPRODUCTION OF THE QUARTERS aboard ships carrying Irish immigrants to Canada. Each family was crammed into a minuscule compartment.

Photograph: Nathalie Legault. "The Crossing of the Irish Immigrants in 1847", exhibit presented by the Marché Bonsecours and the Port of Montreal and produced by le Musée maritime du Québec. Summer 1999.

The journalist Antoine Gérin-Lajoie described the situation:

According to a report published by the Montreal Emigration Committee, almost 100,000 emigrants arrived that year [1847] by way of the Saint Lawrence. Out of that number, 5,293 died at sea, 3,389 at Grosse-Île; 1,137 at Quebec, 3,862 at Montreal, 130 at Lachine, 39 at Saint-Jean: a total of 13,850, without counting those who died in other places in the region, or after they reached Upper Canada or the United States. It is estimated that about a quarter of these people died on their arrival in America ... Unfortunately, the famine that held sway in Ireland that year had bred the fever, and a great number of those who left their homeland were already infected with the disease: the number of deaths during the crossing that before this time were about five per thousand rose in 1847 to 55 per thousand.[1]

In the spring of 1847, it was reported to the Montreal Board of Health that there was a case of typhus among the immigrants who had arrived in the harbour. As ship after ship arrived, the number of typhus cases increased and the mayor of Montreal, John Easton Mills, who was also President of the Immigration Commission, ordered the hasty construction of makeshift sheds to serve as hospitals at Pointe Saint-Charles. Eventually, there were twenty-two such sheds where the sick and the dying were attended by the Sulpician priests and nursed by the Grey Nuns, the Sisters of Providence and the Hôtel-Dieu nuns. Five Sulpicians died, as did seven of the Grey Nuns, three Hôtel-Dieu nuns and three Sisters of Providence. Among the many other victims who died of the disease was John Easton Mills himself.

BISHOP BOURGET'S RESPONSE

In the presence of the calamity facing the city, Ignace Bourget, bishop of Montreal, called in priests from the surrounding countryside to help. In a pastoral letter issued on 13 August 1847, he paid tribute to those who had already died while caring for the sick and exhorted the faithful to find consolation and strength in their faith. Already stricken with the disease himself, the bishop promised that if the city was spared and if he lived he would fulfil three promises. He pledged to restore the practice of pilgrimage to Notre-Dame-de-Bon-Secours Chapel, to present the chapel with a statue of Mary to replace the gift of the baron de Fancamp stolen in 1831 and to commission a votive painting, a memorial of the event, to be placed in the chapel. The bishop lived, the epidemic diminished and, the next year, he kept his promises.

Bishop Bourget had visited Europe in 1841 and 1846 whence he returned greatly impressed by the colourful expressions of piety he had witnessed in Rome. Throughout his episcopate, he was to introduce many Roman practices into his diocese. He thus made sure that the events surrounding the fulfilment of his 1847 promise would be spectacular.

1. Antoine GÉRIN-LAJOIE, *Dix ans au Canada. De 1840 à 1850*, Québec (1888), 438-439, cited in Léon POULIOT, S.J., *Monseigneur Bourget et son temps*, III, *L'évêque de Montréal. Deuxième partie.* Montreal: Bellarmin, 1972, 25.

Le typhus, history of a painting

When Ignace Bourget, Montreal's second bishop, commissioned the Quebec artist, Théophile Hamel, to create a votive painting, the painter already enjoyed an enviable reputation for his portraits of the elite of society, both ecclesiastical and civil. The purpose of the painting was to focus attention on the extraordinary contribution of the religious communities during one of the most tragic events in the history of Montreal, the typhoid epidemic of the summer of 1847. The epidemic began on board the fever ships that carried Irish immigrants fleeing famine in their homeland. To receive the immigrants, about twenty sheds were built on a parcel of land belonging to the Grey Nuns in Pointe Saint-Charles. In their effort to care for the sick, many others contracted the disease, among them, priests and women religious, as well as many lay people.

Bishop Bourget himself became ill on 13 August, the very day that a circular letter addressed to the members of his diocese was published. In it, he recalled the fervour of the first pilgrimages to Notre-Dame-de-Bon-Secours Chapel and made a vow to the Blessed Virgin to restore the practice of making pilgrimage and to donate a new statue to replace the little miraculous statue that had disappeared. Then he added, "I promise you that I will display a votive offering in this sanctuary that you have made your home, a painting representing the typhoid epidemic trying to enter the city but stopped at the gates by your powerful protection."

At the end of autumn 1847, after three years in Europe, Théophile Hamel returned to Montreal. His European training gave him a wider range of subjects. Bishop Bourget's commission became his first and, indeed, his only work based on a national historical event and on religious life in Montreal; moreover, it proved to be his one and only commemorative painting. In it, he repeats the traditional structure that called for a division into two levels. In the upper level, the Blessed Virgin in the clouds is separated from the temporal world found in the lower level. Depicted diagonally from foreground to background are a Grey Nun, a Sister of Providence and a priest administering the last rites to a dying person with the help of a Hôtel Dieu nun. In the background, between the Saint Lawrence and Mount Royal are the city and the bell towers of Notre-Dame. The view from this perspective and the presence of a shed places the scene in its original setting.

Le typhus, commemorative painting by Théophile Hamel circa 1849. This painting at Notre-Dame-de-Bon-Secours Chapel is the oldest Montreal religious painting based on a contemporary event and still exhibited in its original location

Photograph: Bernard Dubois, Marguerite Bourgeoys Museum

The Rescue of the Medusa, painted by Théodore Géricault, Musée du Louvre

Photograph : ©RMN-Arnaudet

In this work, the sick and the dying are partly naked, a rarity in Quebec paintings. Furthermore, the custom of copying elements of other paintings, typical of academic painters, is evident. The two male figures on the extreme right are taken from the famous painting of Géricault, *Le Radeau de la Méduse* (The rescue of the Medusa), (1819) acquired by the Louvre in 1825. Hamel may have sketched this scene when "he went to Paris where he made copies of some of the principal paintings that decorated the famous museums" (*Le courrier du Canada*, 26 December 1870), unless it was copied from an etching. Since most of the drawings and sketches from his portfolio cabinet disappeared in the fire that destroyed his studio in 1862, this point is impossible to verify. And, although it does not measure up to its model, this motif was well chosen to interpret one and the same harsh reality of human misery but, in the Montreal situation, relieved by the help of the religious communities and the clergy.

This painting brought the artist great acclaim at the time, even though it is now regarded as a rather clumsy work. The date of the commemorative painting situates it at the very end of a pictorial style already in decline. Nevertheless, despite weaknesses of composition and technique, *Le typhus* offers a rare and important account of Montreal history that can still be seen at Notre-Dame-de-Bon-Secours.

Jacques Des Rochers, art historian

LA VIERGE DORÉE, statue in gilded bronze moulded in Paris and presented to Notre-Dame-de-Bon-Secours Chapel by Bishop Ignace Bourget in 1848.

Photograph: Monique Tremblay, Marguerite Bourgeoys Museum

On 1 May 1848, Bishop Bourget issued a pastoral letter praising the ancestral devotion to Notre-Dame-de-Bon-Secours and authorizing the Sulpicians to conduct, in the chapel, all the religious exercises suitable to support and encourage pilgrims. On 21 May, the new statue of Mary, intended to replace the tiny madonna given by the baron de Fancamp, was solemnly crowned in Notre-Dame Church. Known as the *Vierge dorée*, this bronze image, slightly more than a metre high, had been commissioned in Paris and depicts the Virgin Mary with arms outspread standing on a globe with the inscription "*Ora pro populo, interveni pro clero*" (Pray for the people, intercede for the clergy). The statue remained in the parish church for the veneration of the faithful throughout the day, then, in the evening, a procession formed to carry it to a place of honour over the altar in Notre-Dame-de-Bon-Secours Chapel. At the Hôtel-Dieu at Saint-Joseph and Saint-Paul streets, a votive heart was presented and hung about the neck of the statue. Many such hearts were presented at this time. The *Vierge dorée* and the votive hearts can still be seen in the chapel today.

In the autumn, a still more striking religious event took place in connection with the chapel. Bishop Bourget decided that the old picture of the Blessed Virgin which had ornamented the wall of the sacristy facing the port would have a more impressive replacement: a statue of Mary, "Star of the Sea", carved by Charles Dauphin, 1.7 metres in height. On 26 September 1848, the bishop issued another pastoral letter announcing his plans:

> This time, it will be on our majestic river that the splendour of one of our most beautiful ceremonies will unfold. You grasp the reason perfectly and you understand that the waters of the ocean must join the earth in making known the glory of Her who brought into the world the Creator of all things.

Early in the morning of Friday, 6 October 1848, a large crowd assembled to participate in a religious event such as Montreal had never before witnessed. In the port lay the steam boats, the *Jacques-Cartier* and the *Saint-Louis,* and the other boats owned by Catholics. The

VOTIVE HEART at Notre-Dame-de-Bon-Secours Chapel containing rolled lists of names from a parish that came in pilgrimage in 1899. These hearts were sometimes engraved with the names of the donors and contained tiny rolls of paper inscribed with individual names or lists of names, prayers and other mementos of the donors and those for whom they prayed.

Photograph: Pierre Fauteux, Marguerite Bourgeoys Museum

LA VIERGE DES MARINS (The Sailors' Madonna), carved in wood, stood on the roof of Notre-Dame-de-Bon-Secours Chapel from 1848 to 1892. It was the work of the Montreal sculptor Charles-Olivier Dauphin (1807-1874) and served to establish his reputation.

Photograph: Françoise Delorme, Marguerite Bourgeoys Museum

new statue could be seen on the upper deck of the *Jacques-Cartier*, raised on a pedestal and surrounded by a guard of honour "as large as the captain's prudence would permit". The bishop and his cortège of clergy and distinguished citizens arrived at eight o'clock and boarded their boat. When the *Veni Creator* was intoned, the singing was taken up by the assembled crowd as the boats sailed across the Saint Lawrence. In front of the Longueuil church the statue was transferred from the *Jacques-Cartier* to the *Saint-Louis*. There the ships turned and made an impressive return across the river as the singing continued and all the bells of the city rang. The statue, mounted on a platform, was carried into Notre-Dame-de-Bon-Secours Chapel by sailors from the various vessels and six captains. On 30 October 1848, the statue was raised to its place on the roof of the chapel overlooking the port of Montreal.

Ignace Bourget, bishop of Montreal

Ignace Bourget whose life spanned most of the nineteenth century had deep roots in the religious past of French Canada: his seventeenth century forbear, Claude Bourget, native of the Beauce region near Chartres, France, had married Marie, daughter of Guillaume Couture, a former *donné* of the Jesuits who had shared the captivity of Isaac Jogues.

The man who became Montreal's second bishop was born in the parish of Saint-Joseph (now Lauzon), Lower Canada, in 1799, the eleventh of thirteen children. He studied at the Petit Séminaire de Québec and at the Séminaire de Nicolet. While still a subdeacon, he was appointed secretary to Jean-Jacques Lartigue, auxiliary bishop at Montreal, who ordained him to the priesthood in November 1822. The young priest was much impressed by Bishop Lartigue's ultramontanist views which he was to share and develop thoughout his life. In 1837, Ignace Bourget was appointed coadjutor to the Bishop of Montreal with the right of succession and on Bishop Lartigue's death in April 1840, he became bishop of Montreal, a diocese that then stretched from the American border to James Bay and from the border with Upper Canada to a line halfway between Quebec and Montreal.

Despite frequent bouts of illness, Bishop Bourget was a man of immense energy and untiring zeal. He set up or helped to set up many enduring institutions: the diocese of Kingston and Bytown (Ottawa), the ecclesiastical province of Quebec and Laval University, to name a few. He relocated and rebuilt Montreal's cathedral after it was destroyed by fire in 1852. In a period of rapid urbanization and growth of the working class, he met the pastoral, educational and social welfare needs of his people by importing several European religious communities, establishing new communities at home and lifting the limit set on the recruitment of established communities like the Congrégation de Notre-Dame de Montréal. Bishop Bourget was a great benefactor of Notre-Dame-de-Bon-Secours Chapel, perhaps in fidelity to his ancestral origins near Chartres, the greatest Marian shrine in France.

Although widely respected as a man of prayer and compassion, Bishop Bourget was also involved in many conflicts. The most important of these was his almost life-long conflict with liberalism, particularly as represented by the Institut Canadien. This influential cultural association, founded in 1844, brought together the young intellectual élite of Montreal to discuss the most advanced ideas of the time and made available in its library books the bishop regarded as dangerous and evil. But Bishop Bourget's policies also involved him in conflict with the Petit Séminaire de Québec and with the Séminaire de

PORTRAIT OF IGNACE BOURGET, second bishop of Montreal. Painting by Soeur Marie-Hélène-de-la-Croix, S.S.A.,13 June 1922.

Photograph: Pierre Costell, 1984. Collection of the Musée des Soeurs de la Providence, Montreal

Saint-Sulpice de Montréal as well as with other members of the Canadian Catholic hierarchy who found his attitudes too intransigent. He retired as bishop of Montreal in September 1876 and died on 8 June 1885 at Sault-au-Recollet.

In Bishop Bourget's funeral oration pronounced at Notre-Dame Church on 12 June 1885, M. Louis Colin, the Superior of the Séminaire de Saint-Sulpice de Montréal described him as "the Bishop who was without question, for the Canadian Church, the most important and the most prodigious man of his century." More than a century later, many would still share this opinion, admirers and detractors alike.

JESUITS AT BON-SECOURS CHAPEL?

In the 1840s, it seemed, for a time, that the Jesuits might assume the direction of Notre-Dame-de-Bon-Secours Chapel. In the second half of the eighteenth century the Jesuits had fallen on black times as their many enemies brought about what seemed to be the final destruction of the community. Expelled from Portugal in September 1759, the Jesuits were suppressed by the Parlement de Paris in August 1762 then dissolved throughout the dominions of the king of France on 1 December 1764. They were expelled from Spain and its possessions in April 1767. Finally, under pressure from the Bourbon kings, they were suppressed by Pope Clement XIV on 21 July 1773. Ironically, they survived in areas ruled by non-Catholic sovereigns, Frederick II in Prussia and Catherine the Great in Russia. By the time the Jesuits were suppressed in the French domains, New France had, of course, passed into the hands of the British and the Jesuits did not completely disappear in Canada until the death of Jean-Joseph Casot, the last surviving member, in 1800, although, like the Recollets, they were not permitted by the British government to recruit new members after 1763.

The Jesuits were re-established by Pope Pius VII in 1814. In 1841, Bishop Bourget sought out their superior general in Rome to ask for Jesuits to conduct a college and to do missionary work among the Amerindians. A group of nine priests arrived in Montreal on 31 May

1842. Since the question of the ownership of the estates the Jesuits had possessed in New France before the Conquest was to drag on for the better part of the century, other arrangements had to be made for their accommodation. In September 1844, under pressure from the bishop, M. Louis-Vincent Quiblier, Superior of the Séminaire de Saint-Sulpice, offered the Jesuits Notre-Dame-de-Bon-Secours Chapel with its yard and neighbouring buildings. The Jesuits, however, found the offer inadequate to their needs, preferring a more peaceful location in the *faubourg* Saint-Antoine and the offer was declined.

In 1847, however, when Bishop Bourget began to plan for the renewal of the chapel as a place of pilgrimage, he again attempted to turn over the chapel to the Jesuits. He suggested that the Sulpicians would be unable to supply the needs of the chapel because they had lost so many of their number in the typhus epidemic. It was with this end in view that he asked the Jesuit superior, Father Félix Martin, to compose the *Manuel du Pèlerin* containing a history of the chapel and suitable devotional material. This work, in which Jacques Viger collaborated, appeared in May 1848. But the Sulpicians were not ready to relinquish the chapel that they had served for so many years and referred the matter to their general assembly. In a letter to the bishop dated 27 November 1847, the superior, M. Pierre-Louis Billaudèle expressed the determination of the Sulpicians to remain in the service of the chapel and its pilgrims. He continued:

> By a privilege of our vocation and our pastoral ministry exercised in a city consecrated to Mary, we are especially devoted to the cult of this divine Mother. How, then, could we give up the consoling service of a Sanctuary so dear to Her Heart, which has come to us by testament, and which we will be happy to be able to pass on to our Successors, just as we have inherited it from our Fathers.

Bishop Bourget's plan to install the Jesuits at Notre-Dame-de-Bon-Secours was abandoned.

THROUGH FIRE AND OTHER CHANGES

Large-scale fires were a regular occurrence during the period of industrialization in cities of the western world without adequate water systems. Montreal was no exception and suffered several fires in the 1850s. On 15 June 1850, a fire that began in a carpenter's shop destroyed more than 200 houses and Saint Stephen's Church. On 23 August, 150 houses were destroyed in half an hour in the area bounded by Craig (now Saint-Antoine), Saint-Laurent, Vitré (now Viger) and Saint-Charles-Borromée (now Clark) streets. On 7 June 1852, a fire which began on *rue* Saint-Pierre burned Saint Andrew's Church and spread as far as Custom House. But the great fire that struck Montreal on 9 July 1852 was one of the most devastating in the history of the city. About 1200 houses were destroyed, most of them built of wood. The population of Montreal was hard hit by this catastrophe that left 10,000 people homeless. This time, however, exceptionally, the religious communities of the old town were spared. The fire started just outside the centre of town in two separate homes in the *faubourgs* Saint-Laurent and Sainte-Marie. The flames threatened to reach Notre-Dame-de-Bon-Secours Chapel but finally stopped just a block short of the building. On the other hand, the cathedral of Saint-Jacques, located in the heart of the blaze on *rue* Saint-Denis, was totally destroyed. While the cathedral was being re-built, the little chapel welcomed the faithful of the district for religious services.

One of the most remarkable features of Old Montreal during this period was the great number of buildings of a religious character. Since their modest beginnings in the seventeenth century, these institutions established in the heart of Montreal had grown to accommodate the needs of the society that they served. The Recollet monastery, the Sulpician seminary, the Hôtel-Dieu, the Hôpital Général and the mother house of the Congrégation de Notre-Dame and their dependencies, with their imposing buildings and large gardens, together covered a considerable area. But for many of these institutions, the days left in Old Montreal were numbered. In the midst of rapid industrial development, there was fierce competition for urban land. A

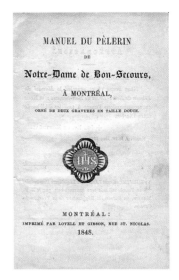

TITLE PAGE OF THE *MANUEL DU PÈLERIN*, written by Félix Martin, S.J., with the collaboration of Jacques Viger, published in 1848.

Marguerite Bourgeoys Museum

"BEHIND BONSECOURS MARKET", oil painting by William Raphael circa 1866. This painter of Prussian origin who attended the Royal Academy of Berlin immigrated to Canada in 1857. This genre painting is meant to be a slightly dramatic portrait of a lively Montreal society, no doubt inspired by romantic German paintings. The great river and the ships in the background, Notre-Dame-de-Bon-Secours — note the long window on the side of the apse that would soon disappear — and Commissioners Street (now de la Commune) make up the backdrop of this animated picture of many colourful characters. The man carrying the satchel under his arm and candelabra in his hand might be the artist himself.

National Gallery of Canada, Ottawa, no. 6673

bitter struggle between tradition and innovation had erupted in the heart of the city. Who would emerge victorious?

In the middle of the century, large economic projects changed the face of Montreal and firmly established the cosmopolitan character of the city. From 1843 to 1849, the Lachine Canal installations were improved to facilitate shipping. Attracted by the hydraulic power provided by the canal, several large industries were established in the area. Nail factories and flour refineries, especially, multiplied.

Farther east, in the old city, Bonsecours Market was erected on the land where the British American Hotel and the Theatre Royal had stood. The work of architect William Footner, the impressive building was designed in the English neo-classical style of Greek inspiration, one of the last examples of this style in Montreal. The city administration had it built, first of all, to house their offices but also with the intention of making of it a multi-purpose building, a vast public market equipped with exhibition rooms and a concert hall. The building was inaugurated in 1847. The offices of the city administration were housed there from 1852 to 1878. This was not the first time that public administration had found a home right next to the chapel, for it was on this very spot, at the Intendance, that François Bigot had stayed whenever he was in Montreal. But, thanks to its great size, its central dome that was generally considered the beacon of Old Montreal and its variety of public functions, Bonsecours Market held a prominent place in the life of Montreal from its very inception. It announced an era of great change in urban architecture. The increase of trade, commerce and industry marked a turning point in the development of Montreal. Here and there in the old city, new, large warehouses sprang up like mushrooms. The control of urban space became a battle over size.

THE GREAT EXODUS

Several of Montreal's venerable institutions found themselves caught between two choices: to move to the greater space available on the outskirts of the city or to remain where they were but to lose part of

BONSECOUR MARKET, Wharves & Montreal.

THE PORT OF MONTREAL, the magnificent Bonsecours Market and Notre-Dame-de-Bon-Secours Chapel before 1893. The statue of the Sailors' Madonna is seen at the top of the chapel.

National Archives of Canada, C-7943

their land. Many of them, though, were left with no other choice really but to pack up and go.

First to leave was Montreal's oldest institution: the Hôtel-Dieu, transferred from *rue* Saint-Paul to Mont Sainte-Famille (now des Pins and Sainte-Famille) in 1861. In 1871, the Hôpital Général was transferred from the site it had occupied since 1693 to Mont Sainte-Croix (now the corner of Guy and René Levesque). The Recollet monastery was a different case for the Recollets no longer existed in Canada. After the Conquest, their church had been shared first with the Anglicans then with the Presbyterians. Their monastery was requisitioned by the British Government for the billeting of troops in November 1796, leaving only the church and a little chapel transformed into a residence for the few surviving Recollets. When Father Louis Demers, the last Recollet priest in Canada, died there on 2 September 1813, the government exercised its right of confiscation to take over the property where the authorities installed a garrison. In 1818, they exchanged it for Île Sainte-Hélène. The new owner sold the monastery and the church to the *fabrique de Notre-Dame* and divided the rest of the property into building lots. This was the church used by the English-speaking Catholics when they became too numerous for Notre-Dame-de-Bon-Secours. Financial considerations forced the selling of the church and monastery in April 1867.

Between 1861 and 1871, then, the buildings of these great institutions were demolished to make way for large warehouses or to extend streets south to the port. The removal did have one advantage for the Grey Nuns and Hospitallers of Saint Joseph: they were able to obtain funds to continue their work through leasing out the buildings on the land they were vacating in the old city. Even the final departure of the military from the *faubourg* Québec in 1871 freed up strategic space for the Canadian Pacific Railway Company to build the city's first two huge grain elevators in 1885. For the time being, the buildings of the Congrégation de Notre-Dame remained, though the community built a new mother house on the Villa Maria property in 1880. Montreal's newly-acquired status as Canada's metropolis paved the way for new commercial enterprises and was used to justify every project, especially if it helped to develop the port industry. All that would survive this major and sudden upheaval were the old Séminaire de Saint-Sulpice, *rue* Notre-Dame, and the oldest part of the Hôpital Général at Pointe-à-Callière, leased to tradesmen. Economic pressure, noise and pollution led the other institutions to re-locate to the outskirts of the city, though not without regret, "shedding many tears", wrote a sister of the Hôtel-Dieu. Some of the population saw these moves as a signal for them to leave as well. The middle class and the craftsmen abandoned Old Montreal to tradesmen and manufacturers

THE HÔPITAL GÉNÉRAL ON ITS ORIGINAL SITE at Pointe-à-Callière in Old Montreal before it was torn down in 1872 to open up Saint-Pierre and Normant streets. Fortunately, the oldest part of the building was saved. The construction of the old hospital by the Frères Charon goes back to 1693. Owned by the Grey Nuns since 1747, the historic building is known today as the Maison de Mère d'Youville.

Archives of the Sœurs Grises de Montréal

and to labourers, more often than not the poorest members of society.

It would seem inevitable that in the 1860s Notre-Dame-de-Bon-Secours Chapel, with its statue of Our Lady turned toward the harbour, must be caught in the wake of "progress". Located at the bottom of *rue* Saint-Denis, the chapel occupied a site that could easily become a link between the city and the port, an important link since the economic growth of Montreal depended, to a large extent, on the movement of traffic between the city and its totally new port installations. And so, it seemed as if the chapel stood in the way of an access road to the port.

The little landing area that had served Montreal until the early 1830s had become a harbour equipped with impressive wharfs and piers that were now able to accommodate the large steamships that docked in increasing numbers to load and unload merchandise. All along *rue* de la Commune, Commissioners Street at the time, new greystone warehouses sprang up, built by companies to facilitate the transfer of cargo. In the opinion of some people, the way to the rapid growth of Montreal could be summed up in a single word: demolish. Directly in line with *rue* Bonsecours/Saint-Denis, Notre-Dame-de-Bon-Secours Chapel, in its turn, attracted the attention of municipal authorities in 1863. That year, a city inspector was commissioned by the Roads Committee to approach the *fabrique* of Notre-Dame about the possibility of buying the Bonsecours lands so that the street could be extended to the port. An exchange of letters between the *fabrique* and the city and notarized acts kept in the archives of the *fabrique* of Notre-Dame offer an account of this episode.

The result of this operation would certainly have been the destruction of the chapel. The idea gradually gained ground since, four years later, the wardens seemed ready to cede the property to the municipal corporation for an undetermined sum of money. When Marguerite Bourgeoys asked that Notre-Dame-de-Bon-Secours be annexed to the parish of Notre-Dame in 1678, she had made one point very clear: the annexation contract indicated that the site on which the chapel had been built was to be consecrated to Mary "in perpetuity".

Neither the Sulpicians nor the Congrégation de Notre-Dame was willing, however, to see Montreal left without a chapel of pilgrimage dedicated to Notre-Dame-de-Bon-Secours and the decision was made that, if the existing chapel disappeared, it would be rebuilt on a different site. Because it was judged that the *fabrique* of Notre-Dame did not have the financial resources to undertake such a project, it was arranged that the Sulpicians would buy the chapel on the understanding that they were committed to its rebuilding.

The act of sale of 1869 made the Sulpicians the new owners of the chapel in exchange for a 40,000 dollar reduction of the debt of the *fabrique* to the seminary. The notarized approval of this sale by the sisters confirmed the role of the Congregation as protector of the chapel in the name of its founder. Sisters of the Congrégation de Notre-Dame, represented by Sister Sainte-Ursule, (Mary Ann Gibson), Superior General, renewed this intention of the founder and the terms of its renewal before the notary, E. Lafleur, in June 1870:

> With what great satisfaction did they learn that, by deed of sale contracted in the presence of the undersigned notary on 8 September last, the Séminaire de St-Sulpice de Montréal acquired from the *fabrique* de *Notre-Dame de Ville-Marie de Montréal* the land and the chapel or church of Notre Dame de Bonsecours in this city since this sale ensures more than ever that the wishes and intentions of their foundress, Sister Bourgeoys, will be carried out: she who, in making this donation to the *fabrique*, had no other intention than to ensure its survival and its dependence on the parish of Notre-Dame de Ville-Marie in perpetuity; and how much more so since the new plans of this City to extend *rue* Bonsecours down to the St. Lawrence River would involve the demolition and disappearance of the said church, it is very probable that the said *fabrique* could not or would not want to rebuild it, while the Seminary, on the contrary, acquired it with the intention of rebuilding it on the neighbouring property that it has purchased to this end.

This notarized approval is far from being of secondary importance. The document shows to what extent the sisters of the Congrégation de Notre-Dame had recognized rights over the fate of the chapel, even if they did not own it. From the time of the foundation of the chapel in the seventeenth century, they have remained the moral legatees, confirmed by the writings of their foundress, Marguerite Bourgeoys.

As for the extension of *rue* Saint-Denis to the port, it looks as if the city abandoned the project somewhere along the way. The opening up of *rue* Saint-Pierre and *rue* Normant on the western edge of Old Montreal in 1871 and 1872 had already established an important connection between the city and the port. A quarter of a century later, the mother house of the Congrégation de Notre-Dame would have to be sacrificed to permit the extension of boulevard Saint-Laurent down to the port area.

THE CHAPEL AND THE PAPAL ZOUAVES

Given the ultramontanist sympathies of Bishop Bourget, it is scarcely surprising that Canadians became involved in the struggle to defend the independence of the Papal States during the campaign for the unification of Italy. At a moment when it was not easy to distinguish the temporal from the spiritual power of the Pope, enrolling "under the standard of the Holy Father" appeared a noble and heroic act. Among those already enrolled in the Papal Army in the early 1860s was Benjamin-Antoine Testard de Montigny, great-great grandson of Jacques Testard de Montigny. In October 1867, in the face of an ever worsening situation, Pius IX addressed an encyclical to the bishops of the world. In it, he described the impossibility of his position and recommended himself to the prayers of the faithful. The response in several European countries was to assume the cost of sending contingents of men to join the papal army known as the Zouaves. This name had been given them by General La Moricière who had commanded Zouaves in Africa before taking over the papal army in 1860. Under the inspiration of Bishop Bourget, seven contingents of Papal Zouaves, more than 500 men, were to leave Canada for Italy between 1868 and 1870.

MINIATURE SILVER SHIP commemorating the safe return from Italy of the Papal Zouaves in 1870 and symbolizing their attachment to the Church, "the barque of Peter", presented to the chapel in thanksgiving in 1872. The ship contained a wooden cylinder holding a scroll with the inscription: "Love God and go your way. Names of the Canadian Papal Zouaves who subscribed to the maintenance in perpetuity of the votive lamp in Notre Dame de Bonsecours." There follows a list of sixty-nine names.

Photograph: Rachel Gaudreau, Marguerite Bourgeoys Museum

On 20 September 1870, the siege of Rome came to an end when the pope decided to surrender rather than risk a blood bath. The agreement made with the opposing force contained the provision that the Zouaves would be transported to the border of their respective countries. For a time, it seemed that the island of Elba was to be considered the border of Canada! However, it was agreed that all British subjects would be transported to Liverpool at the expense of the British government and on 1 October 1870, the Canadians were put aboard ship at Livorno. The voyage was difficult: the men were dressed only in their prisoners' uniforms, many were ill with fever and the hurricane season had begun. They were hit by so severe a storm that it took ten days to reach Liverpool.

On 19 October, the returning Canadian Zouaves boarded the American ship, the *Idaho*, for New York. Philias Bleau, one of their number, wrote about the voyage:

At sea we had a terrible storm that lasted three days. We thought we would die. But Notre-Dame de Bon Secours to whom we prayed protected us. We promised her an *ex-voto*, and a visit to her church as soon as we reached home. We arrived in Montreal toward the evening of 12 November (1870) where a supper was awaiting us at the parish reading room of the Gentlemen of St. Sulpice. We made our visit to Notre-Dame de Bon Secours Chapel. We promised to have a miniature replica of the *Idaho* made to bring to this Chapel.[2]

The miniature silver ship commemorating the *Idaho* was presented to the chapel on 26 May 1872. Along with other votive offerings, it hangs there still. The Zouaves received a tumultuous welcome on their return to Montreal. Of the 506 men who had served, nine had died. Many of the returnees would later have distinguished careers, among them Louis-Philippe Hébert, the sculptor responsible for the Maisonneuve monument in Place d'Armes. The standard blessed and presented to the first Zouave contingent to leave Montreal in 1868 was placed for a time in Notre-Dame-de-Bon-Secours Chapel. In 1894, this standard, together with various mementoes of the Zouaves and tablets recording their names, was placed in a side chapel of Saint-Jacques-le-Majeur Cathedral (now Marie-Reine-du-Monde). There they remain to this day.

A TRAIN STATION INSTEAD OF A CHAPEL

Though Marguerite Bourgeoys left no written explanation for her choice of the site for Notre-Dame-de-Bon-Secours Chapel, it is easy to imagine that she chose it because of its geographic advantage, a small promontory visible from the river, close to the town, accessible both by water and by land: everything that could be hoped for, ideal for a pilgrimage site. At the end of the nineteenth century, trapped in the port expansion with the railway creeping up, the little promontory and its chapel were hanging on by a thread.

Ever since the opening of the Victoria Bridge in 1860 provided the signal for the expansion of the railway network on the island of Montreal to link up with the port installations, it was foreseeable that soon a central railway station would be needed. The old site of the

2. Cited in Annette BLEAU, "Philias Bleau, Zouave pontifical", *Cahiers de la Société historique de Montréal*, vol. 2, nos. 2 and 3 (mars/juin, 1983), 116-117.

barracks, which the city bought back from the Canadian government in 1874 and immediately turned over to a railway company to serve the port of Montreal, had already prepared the way. Once the barracks were knocked down and tracks were laid, a railway station was needed; and in 1882, the die seemed to be cast. The city planned to expropriate the chapel with the intention of re-designing that part of town to build a central station and warehouses and to facilitate container traffic between the station and the port. Both Protestant and Catholic groups were incensed, contested the decision before the city council and brought their case to the newspapers, rejecting the economic arguments presented by the authorities. They countered concern for the economy with the duty of remembrance and respect for history; they proposed continuity and tradition instead of the rise of uncontrolled progress. In his *Histoire de Notre-Dame-de-Bon-Secours*, Jean-Marie Leleu presents numerous accounts of these firm defenders, expressed in patriotic language whose tone, though perhaps somewhat colourful for modern taste, was very much in keeping with the spirit of the times. In the end, the opponents of this plan for the railway won their case and Dalhousie Station was built on *rue Berri*.

So, despite the urban and harbour development that marked this period, the little chapel kept its ancient place and, in accord with the intentions of Bishop Bourget, continued to draw great crowds who came in pilgrimage or to hear the important preachers of the day who spoke to them in the chapel. Not only did it escape demolition: it was on the verge of a new period of growth and embellishment.

A PILGRIMAGE OF THE PAPAL ZOUAVES to Notre-Dame-de-Bon-Secours Chapel in 1999. The Papal Zouaves continue to exist, although only the Valleyfield group remains very active. It meets weekly for musical and military exercises and helps with various parish activities. The pilgrimage of the Zouaves to the chapel takes place each September.

Photograph: Monique Tremblay, Marguerite Bourgeoys Museum

CHAPTER 5

SPLENDOUR AND DECLINE (1883-1968)

ALTHOUGH NOTRE-DAME-DE-BON-SECOURS did not give way under the tidal wave of urban development that engulfed Montreal in the second half of the nineteenth century, it was, however, caught up in a huge vortex of transformations and renovations. These transformations can be attributed in large part to the chaplain, Hugues Rolland *dit* Lenoir, S.S., who was determined to modernize the building. But the lovely chapel on *rue* Saint-Paul was far from being the only project of a religious nature on the order books of artists and architects. For this period was marked by important changes on the Montreal ecclesiastical scene.

MONTREAL, CITY OF A HUNDRED SPIRES

Until after the middle of the nineteenth century, Notre-Dame continued to be Montreal's sole parish. With few exceptions, the Montreal priests lived at the Séminaire de Saint-Sulpice which they left each day for the various auxiliary churches and chapels. Certain ceremonies — baptisms, marriages, the reception of Easter communion — could take place only in the parish church. By 1864 Notre-Dame had about 100,000 parishioners. In 1865, after a long struggle with the Sulpicians who wished to keep the parish intact, Bishop Bourget succeeded in persuading the Sacred Congregation of Propaganda in Rome to authorize the division of Notre-Dame Parish. Between September 1866 and December 1867, the bishop erected ten new canonical parishes. Though legal difficulties remained in the civil sphere and the struggle over what was called the "dismemberment of the parish" was by no means over, the creation of new parishes did lead in the next decades to a great period of church building in Montreal so that it came to be known as the "city of the hundred spires".

The increase in the population of Montreal, and so of its church-goers, and the economic boom of the period had inevitable consequences in the religious sphere. The rivalry among Catholics, Anglicans and Protestants often found expression in art and architecture and in a profusion of construction and renovation projects. Notre-Dame-de-Bon-Secours Chapel was not to be left behind in this "battle of the steeples", fought primarily in the area of artistic expression.

SWEEPING CHANGES AT NOTRE-DAME-DE-BON-SECOURS

It was in this climate of optimism that the Sulpicians planned the transformation of Notre-Dame-de-Bon-Secours. The very simple architectural design of the building — perhaps too simple for romantic Victorians — and its dilapidated state, a constant reminder of its more than a hundred years of existence, called for a transformation that would silence detractors once and for all. Moreover, Montreal was fast approaching the celebration of the 250th anniversary of its founding (1892) and it was judged that the little chapel should reflect the fashion of the day.

M. Lenoir, responsible for the renovation project in 1885, had already overseen the building of Notre-Dame-de-Lourdes Chapel (1875-1882) in the Saint-Jacques district of Montreal and so had the necessary experience. The architects Perrault and Mesnard, appointed to plan and execute the renovations, initially submitted three proposals. The first of these suggested keeping the exterior walls, advancing the central façade marginally and extending the back of the chapel toward Commissioners Street. The interior decoration of the chapel would remain unchanged. The second proposal suggested keeping the side walls and re-building everything else. The last proposal suggested the total demolition of the existing building and its reconstruction on the same site with an east-west orientation along *rue* Saint-Paul instead of the actual north-south orientation. The accepted proposal was the middle ground between the first proposal and the second since everything was re-done, but without going so far as to destroy the original.

The plan decided on was as follows. On the inside, a new Roman vault would be constructed of timbered wood that would cover the ceiling decorated by the sculptor Louis-Xavier Leprohon in 1823. The exterior would be graced with a new stone façade built up against the old one, thus hiding some of the original features such as the central circular window, the large arched windows and the cut-stone cross in the gable. The new façade conceived by the architects would include a double-lanterned steeple, two lateral pinnacles and a projecting portal surmounted by a cornice containing a statue of the Blessed Virgin.

THE VAULT OF NOTRE-DAME-DE-BON-SECOURS DECORATED BY FRANÇOIS-ÉDOUARD MELOCHE. The transformation of the interior décor of the chapel was a significantly large undertaking as the two photographs show, the one taken just before the work began in 1886 and the other between 1888 and 1893.

Archives nationales du Québec, Quebec, P600,S6,PN80-4-21

Notman photographic archives, McCord Museum of Canadian History, Montreal, view 1320

BETHELEEM, the painting done by Meloche in trompe l'oeil at Notre-Dame-de-Bon-Secours that is the most directly inspired by Julius Schnorr's illustrated Bible.

Photograph: Alain Laforest

The Schnorr illustrated Bible, 1860 edition, facsimile 1988; archives of the Marguerite Bourgeoys Museum

A VAULT DECORATED IN TROMPE L'ŒIL

To decorate the interior, M. Lenoir hired François-Xavier-Édouard Meloche, an artist whose skill he admired and whom he had seen at work at Notre-Dame-de-Lourdes Chapel. Student of the painter, sculptor and architect, Napoléon Bourassa, Meloche had learned from his teacher the use of the very distinctive trompe l'oeil décor that would soon become his personal signature. Before Bonsecours, Meloche had already completed the interior decoration and ornamentation of a dozen churches. Sainte-Madeleine of Coteau-du-Lac (1881), Notre-Dame-de-la-Visitation in Champlain (1881-1882) and Saint-Michel in Vaudreuil (1883) were among his most notable commissions.

At Notre-Dame-de-Bon-Secours Chapel, Meloche painted a sequence of eight scenes illustrating the life of the Blessed Virgin directly on the wooden laths of the vault. He took his inspiration for the narrative structure and the composition of certain of the paintings from the Bible illustrated by the German artist, Julius Schnorr von Carolsfeld, whose 1860 English edition or 1883 abridged Anglo-German edition was probably familiar to Meloche. Meloche had been well prepared by the master, Napoléon Bourassa, who followed the pictorial style of the German group known as the Nazarenes. Meloche was likely familiar with the decorative style of the église du Gesù in Montreal executed in a similar vein by the New Yorker Daniel Müller in 1865. The eight scenes painted on the Bon-Secours vault take up the traditional themes of Marian iconography: the Nativity of Mary, the Presentation of Mary in the Temple, the Espousals of Mary and Joseph, the Annunciation, the Visitation, the Nativity of Jesus, the Presentation of Jesus in the Temple, the life of the Holy Family in Nazareth. Completed in trompe l'œil, the vault of the nave is painted in shades of rose, turquoise and grey and accented in gold, a relatively monochromatic palette. For the central medallion on the vault of the sanctuary, the crowning of Mary, the artist chose a palette with a brighter rose. The painting is surrounded by angels and cherubs.

François-Édouard Meloche

François-Édouard Meloche, son of a well-to-do Montreal clockmaker, succeeded brilliantly at his studies at the Jesuit Collège Sainte-Marie in Montreal; however, his father's prolonged illness plunged the family into debt, forcing the young Meloche to abandon his studies to meet his own financial needs and those of his family. Doing a hundred and one small jobs to earn a living, Meloche soon attracted the attention of Napoléon Bourassa who took him under his wing and taught him painting, sculpture and architecture. Under the instruction of the master, Meloche completed his artistic training with the ornamentation of Notre-Dame-de-Lourdes Chapel (1872-1882). In all likelihood, this chapel was, after the église du Gesù (1865), the second Montreal establishment whose interior was decorated in trompe l'oeil in the spirit of the Nazarenes. From the beginning of his artistic output, Meloche drew his inspiration for the decoration of church interiors from the Nazarene group.[1] This German school developed in the nineteenth century, influenced by artists of the Italian Renaissance such as Raphael, as well as by the style of Albrecht Dürer.

One of the dominant figures of this school of art, Julius Schnorr von Carolsfeld, absorbed the Italian and German styles of the two artists whom he had chosen to emulate. To some extent, Schnorr and his group invented a new style whose narrative thread was derived from Bible themes. The German artist published a first edition of his illustrated Bible in 1851, followed by an English translation in 1860. This Bible served as a reference work for many nineteenth-century artists, Meloche among them. Unlike Daniel Müller who faithfully copied the Bible scenes to decorate the Gesù, at Notre-Dame-de-Bon-Secours, Meloche modified Schnorr's scenes to suit his own personal style.

In the course of his career, Meloche decorated about forty churches in Canada. His use of trompe l'oeil, rosettes, garlands and mouldings gives depth to the buildings in which the technique is used. "Meloche proves that he is a great muralist: the ornamentation alone is the entire décor. ... As for the narrative content, the Schnorr Bible and other sources, it was his private hunting preserve, the secret of his ability as a painter of pictures."[2] As well as a painter of murals, Meloche was a sculptor and architect, the recipient of a prestigious award for his decorative architecture and painted interiors: a medal at the World's Columbian Exposition held in Chicago in 1893. His works were also awarded a prize at the Paris World's Fair in 1900 at a time when his career was already in decline. François-Édouard Meloche died in relative obscurity in 1914 at the age of fifty-eight.

THE CHERUB, the graphic signature used by Meloche in his decoration of church interiors.

Photograph: Rachel Gaudreau, Marguerite Bourgeoys Museum

1. This information on Meloche and the Nazarenes is taken from an unpublished manuscript by Adriana A. Davies entitled "François-Édouard Meloche: The Last Nazarene".
2. Cécile BELLEY, "François-Édouard Meloche (1855-1914) muraliste et professeur, et le décor de l'église Notre-Dame-de-la-Visitation de Champlain", Master's thesis, Concordia University, 1989, 112-113.

THE GUARDIAN ANGEL, one of
the dozen wooden statues signed
Gratton and Laperle, 1890.

Photograph: Monique Tremblay,
Marguerite Bourgeoys Museum

On the Notre-Dame-de-Bon-Secours worksite, Meloche surrounded himself with artists and artisans some of whom, like his
foreman Toussaint-Xénophon Renaud, were former colleagues who
had studied with him at the Notre-Dame-de-Lourdes building-site
school. One of the paintings is signed in pencil "fecit W Lorenz
1886".[3] It is not impossible that this artisan was one of Meloche's
students. In fact, Meloche taught painting at the école du Conseil des
arts et manufactures de la province de Québec in Montreal from 1886
to 1899. Did he take his students to his work sites to give them
practice as his former teacher had done? It is certainly conceivable
since he was known to use the same teaching methods as Bourassa. In
class, as in his own work, Meloche carried on the artistic methods of
his teacher.

Referring to Notre-Dame-de Lourdes, Napoléon Bourassa spoke
of the "mathematics of painting" to explain the harmony that must
exist between the choice of colours and pictorial forms and the architecture of the place. It is obvious that Meloche took this lesson to
heart. He too had the ability to create harmony between his decorative motifs and the interior space to bring to the fore the architectural
characteristics of the building. From one church to the next, Meloche
succeeded in creating a judicious integration of architectural style and
interior ornamentation through his decorative motifs, his choice of
tones and his geometric composition. Even if the inspiration for his
iconographic themes was derived from the Schnorr illustrated Bible,
Meloche was not just a copyist. Today, apart from Notre-Dame-de-
Bon-Secours Chapel where Meloche's work has been re-discovered
thanks to recent restorations, the most remarkable examples of his
talent are to be found outside Montreal in such churches as Saint-
Michel in Vaudreuil, Saint-Philippe-Apôtre in Saint-Philippe d'Argen-
teuil or Sainte-Marie in Sainte-Marie-de-Beauce.

Until 1890, the furnishings of the chapel and a number of its
other architectural elements were still being changed. In the words of
M. Lenoir himself, it was time to give back to the chapel the respect
it deserved as a place of pilgrimage to the Blessed Virgin, rather than

3. This observation was made
by Patrick Legris' team of
restorers in 1997 during the
chapel renovations.

to let it be "an old curiosity shop." The chaplain was referring especially to the baldaquin designed by Joseph Pépin and Louis-Amable Quévillon that came from the old Notre-Dame Church and that he now replaced with a monumental wooden altar. Twelve wooden statues were ordered from the sculptors Joseph-Olindo Gratton and Marie-Philippe-Richard Banlier *dit* Laperle, at the time partners under the name of Gratton et Laperle. For the main altar, they designed eight angels of adoration, a Saint Michael Archangel and a guardian angel; for the two niches in the pillars of the sanctuary, a Saint Joachim and a Saint Anne. The sanctuary windows were totally changed. The two large, arched, side windows trimmed with stained glass were replaced by a series of three circular windows built into the upper part of the wall. The eight windows of the nave were decorated in grisaille, a kind of monochrome paint that matched the vault. The floor was renovated and the benches of the nave were replaced. The lighting underwent a small transformation, converted as it was from candlelight to gas lamps and soon replaced by electric lighting.

THE "STAR OF THE SEA"

Once the decoration of the chapel was completed, M. Lenoir once again called upon Meloche, this time to use his architectural skills to plan a façade overlooking the port. The little chapel, originally planned in the French style, was transformed into a chapel with an impressively large exterior, very Victorian in style. To understand this radical change, it is important to realize what was happening around the chapel at the time. The city had expropriated land to widen Commissioners Street behind the chapel in order to promote the port expansion and to build large wharves, all of which required the demolition of several buildings. Thus, in 1891, the back of the chapel was cut off from the building housing the sacristy and the school to the east and the Brodeur building that stood to the west of the apse. The little stalls of the vendors along the west wall were torn down and the stone wall of the chapel was covered with a layer of

THE STAR OF THE SEA
Archives of
Marguerite Bourgeoys Museum

ORIGINAL DRAWING OF THE
FAÇADE OF THE CHAPEL ON THE
RIVER SIDE, bearing the inscription, "Monument of N.D. de
Bonsecours - Built to commemo-
rate the 250th anniversary of the
founding of Ville-Marie. F.Ed.
Meloche author of the plans
1892." Trans.

Archives of the Congrégation de
Notre-Dame de Montréal

NUMBER 2 GRAIN ELEVATOR
OPPOSITE THE CHAPEL around the
1920s. The building was torn
down in 1978 to open up a
"window onto the river."

National Archives of Canada,
PA61417

L'Accueil Bonneau

L'Accueil Bonneau, located next to Notre-Dame-de-Bon-Secours Chapel since 1904, has been directed by the Grey Nuns of Montreal from its foundation. This institution keeps alive in Old Montreal a tradition of social assistance begun in the nineteenth century by the Sulpicians and Bishop Bourget, as well as by a number of philanthropic lay people who played an active role.

One of the latter, Joseph Vincent, a boat owner, founded the Hospice Saint-Charles in 1877 with the help of the Sulpicians and the Grey Nuns. The institution was housed originally in the barracks in the *faubourg* Québec abandoned by the military when the garrison left. After a number of moves, the mission settled at Champ de Mars in 1895 under the name *Fourneau économique* (soup kitchen), and was supported financially by the Sulpicians and the Saint Vincent-de-Paul Society of Montreal. But a growing clientèle made a further move necessary. The Sulpicians owned a row of seven stores built of stone next to Notre-Dame-de-Bon-Secours Chapel on what is now *rue* de la Commune. They offered the institution first two and then the entire seven stores that had previously been rented by fruit and vegetable sellers. L'Accueil Bonneau, at the time called the "*Œuvre des sans-foyer, le Vestiaire des Pauvres*", came into being.

The heart and soul of the institution at the time was Rose-de-Lima Bonneau, S.G.M., a legendary figure in this part of Old Montreal, who looked out for the itinerant population. Sister Bonneau remained at the *Vestiaire* from 1909 until her death in 1934. In 1968, the *Vestiaire des Pauvres* on *rue* de la Commune became l'Accueil Bonneau in her honour and memory. The Grey Nuns of Montreal continue to play an active role in the institution to this day, providing care to the homeless and the destitute.

cement, the first alteration it had seen since its construction in 1771. The old *Friponne* warehouse was demolished at the same time as the building east of the apse. In 1893, the Sulpicians, who had owned the property since the threat of demolition in 1869, rebuilt a row of stores, somewhat set back from the street and partly over the founda-tions of *la Friponne*. The Accueil Bonneau, an institution serving the homeless of the area under the direction of the Grey Nuns of Montreal, has been located there since 1903. The building that sheltered the Accueil was completely destroyed in 1998 by a gas explosion but was reconstructed within months in the same architectural style.

The demolition of the old buildings was seen as an opportunity to do something new and to freshen up the image of the chapel as an integral part of an expanding port. The chapel renovations were carried out at the same time as the Canadian Pacific Railway was building its huge wooden grain elevators in the *faubourg* Québec and only a few years before the gigantic port installations of 1900 with their immense piers and sheds and the two cement grain elevators built along Commissioners Street (de la Commune). The symbolism of the "Star of the Sea," begun in the previous century with a modest outdoor painting and replaced in 1848 by the wooden statue over the apse donated by Bishop Bourget, took on totally different proportions after 1892. Certainly, the chapel's location at the very entrance to the harbour gave it a prominent position in the Montreal landscape.

Under the impetus of M. Lenoir, who saw this project as an opportunity to create a symbolic house of Nazareth, Meloche built an impressive tower over the apse of the chapel on whose summit would stand an image of Mary almost eight metres high. This true "Star of the Sea", radiant in a crown of light and visible from afar, would extend welcoming and protecting arms to everyone entering or leaving the harbour. The central part of the tower that supports the statue of Mary was covered by a shell-pattern copper roof and endowed with a lantern lookout. It is flanked on either side by square towers, each enhanced with a pavilion-like roof, and surmounted by an angel with spread wings blowing a trumpet. The contract for the statuary was granted to the former partner of Olindo Gratton, Philippe Laperle, who created the colossal statue of Mary as well as eight adoring angels, two angels with trumpets and the three theological virtues of Faith, Hope and Charity. In Montreal at the time, this ambitious project was without equal except for the construction of the cathedral Saint-Jacques-le-Majeur (known today as Marie-Reine-du-Monde).

THE TOWER DESIGNED BY MELOCHE BETWEEN 1892 AND 1894. In this photograph taken in the first half of the twentieth century, the statue of one of the theological virtues, Faith, has already been removed from its base.

Fonds Massicotte, Pharon Collection, Bibliothèque nationale du Québec, DS6/1363

THE HEAD OF ONE OF THE THREE THEOLOGICAL VIRTUES, probably Hope, found in the cellar of the chapel in 1997. This work of Philippe Laperle was restored by the *Centre de conservation du Québec*.

Photograph: Pierre Fauteux
Marguerite Bourgeoys Museum

4. Cécile BELLEY, "François-Édouard Meloche (1855-1914) muraliste et professeur, et le décor de l'église Notre-Dame-de-la-Visitation-de-Champlain," Master's thesis, Concordia University, 1989, 114-115.

For the chapel in the tower, M. Lenoir had commissioned a replica of the Holy House of Loretto to be built in Italy. (According to legend, this was the home of the Holy Family in Nazareth miraculously transported to Italy in the thirteenth century). The chapel consecrated to the Holy Family even had a thoroughly modern elevator, installed in 1893, to facilitate access to it by the greatest possible number of visitors. On the lower levels under the tower, the reconstruction of the buildings behind Bon-Secours Chapel presented an opportunity to erect a stone building three storeys high to house a new sacristy and school rooms where the Sisters of the Congrégation de Notre-Dame would teach. Finally, on 9 September 1894, feast, that year, of the Holy Name of Mary, a grand ceremony attracting 20,000 people was organized to bless what can arguably be called a monument to the glory of Mary. The archbishop of Montreal, Édouard-Charles Fabre, celebrated Mass and the day closed with an act of consecration of the city of Montreal to the Blessed Virgin.

RE-DECORATED AGAIN ... IN THE STYLE OF THE DAY!

After its popularity in the second half of the nineteenth century, trompe l'oeil was severely castigated by critics of art and architecture from the outset of the twentieth. Hardly twenty years after Meloche had applied the first brush stroke to the vault of Notre-Dame-de-Bon-Secours Chapel, trompe l'oeil was considered a breach of good taste. Art critics were not sparing in their negative comments: the Sulpician Olivier Maurault linked it to falsehood; Pierre-Georges Roy, archivist for the province of Quebec, spoke of the absolute mess created at Notre-Dame-de-Bon-Secours and, to cap it all, the historian Gérard Morisset pronounced himself amazed that "religious art" could be so easily "debased that it became a cheap commodity of showy stuff, trite, inane and sugary."[4] Now that trompe l'oeil was in disrepute, it was necessary to wipe out every trace of this embarrassing artistic form and give the chapel a more modern sheen. In 1908, the die was cast.

The decorative artist Delphis-Adolphe Beaulieu was commissioned to completely refurbish the interior ornamentation. He was supposed to wash the paintings on the vaults and put four coats of paint over them to obliterate the work of Meloche forever. But Beaulieu used another technique, the result of which would preserve almost intact the décor painted on the wooden laths. Rather than paint on the wood surface, he instead glued canvas directly to the vault of the nave and sanctuary over the paintings of Meloche. His decorative motif, of great geometric simplicity, was painted on the canvas in shades of blue and off-white. The effect was much brighter than before and this, no doubt, was what he was aiming for. The

THE VAULT OF THE CHAPEL REDECORATED in 1908 by D.A. Beaulieu who painted on canvas that was then glued to the vault.

Archives of the Marguerite Bourgeoys Museum

Ozias Leduc

In 1908, Delphis-Adolphe Beaulieu (1849-1928), a
Montreal painter, was commissioned to re-decorate Notre-
Dame-de-Bon-Secours Chapel. He sub-contracted the work
of painting several pictures to Ozias Leduc (1864-1955).[5]
At that time, the Saint-Hilaire painter had already deco-
rated several chapels and churches in Quebec, in the
Maritime provinces and in New England.

PAINTING OF MARGUERITE
BOURGEOYS BY OZIAS LED

Photograph: Rachel Gaudreau
Marguerite Bourgeoys Museur

In April 1909, Beaulieu asked Leduc to create commemorative paintings of Marguerite Bourgeoys and of Paul de
Chomedey de Maisonneuve. These oval-shaped medallions
were to ornament the walls of the chapel on either side of
the entrance. As they were to be historical portraits, the artist
would have to take his inspiration from real or imagined
portraits of the subjects. Beaulieu informed him that he would
furnish a picture of Marguerite Bourgeoys, but stated that he
had not been able to find any likeness of the founder of
Montreal.

The religious picture of Marguerite Bourgeoys given to Leduc has been
printed many times in different sizes, with or without the text. The engraving
used for this picture was done in the workshop of Ch. Letaille, engraver,
lithographer and editor of religious pictures, active in Paris between 1840 and
1876. The picture shows Marguerite Bourgeoys and her companions kneeling
before an altar on which are placed a crucifix and a statue of the Virgin and
Child. The text that sometimes accompanies the picture is based on a quota-
tion from the writings of Marguerite Bourgeoys, "Divine wisdom is seen in
this: that one reflects on the life and actions of the Blessed Virgin in order to
imitate her as closely as possible." The scene and the text call to mind the
great devotion of the founder to Our Lady, but they also recall Marguerite's
wisdom, one of the Christian virtues that her companions recognized in her.
This picture, with the accompanying text, was probably produced between
1878 and 1880 after Marguerite was declared "venerable" by the Church, as
it is entitled "*Venerable* Sister Marguerite Bourgeoys". This idealized image of
Mother Bourgeoys no doubt met with the approval of the Sisters of the
Congrégation de Notre-Dame whose intention it was to have the holiness of
their founder recognized. Distributing this picture to their students allowed the
Sisters to incite them to piety and moral standards. The portrait painted by
Ozias Leduc is a close reproduction of the religious picture. The artist merely

THIS IS THE PRINT ON WHICH
OZIAS LEDUC based his painting
of Marguerite Bourgeoys.
Maison Letaille, Paris

5. The documentation concerning
the involvement of Ozias Leduc at
Notre-Dame-de-Bon-Secours Chapel is preserved in the Ozias Leduc
collection of the Bibliothèque
nationale du Québec.

framed the scene more tightly, bringing it up into the foreground, made the crucifix smaller and used drapery to enclose the space.

Leduc would be much more creative in painting the portrait of Monsieur de Maisonneuve. Since Beaulieu had not given him a picture with which to work, Leduc probably consulted the biography written by the Sulpician Pierre Rousseau and published in 1886. An engraved portrait appears on the frontispiece. Its origin is still unknown and it authenticity has been questioned since the end of the nineteenth century. Referring to this portrait in his book entitled "*Portraits des héros de la Nouvelle-France — Images d'un culte historique*", Denis Martin wrote, "This quiet and sober face lent itself easily enough to the description of the heroic and religious virtues of the founder of Montreal." And he cited in support the analysis of Rousseau, the biographer, "The face breathes intelligence, but especially goodness and serenity … There is in it a charm that invites confidence and respect, it is the reflection of a pure and modest heart, shy perhaps …" In his portrait, Ozias Leduc respects this idealized view and even accentuates it. Drawing his inspiration from the etching, he nevertheless puts it through several transformations: from a bust portrait of a subject seen in three-quarter view and turned to the right, he paints the upper half of the subject as far as the belt, thus moving the scene back somewhat; moreover, the subject faces left, no doubt so that his back is not turned to Marguerite Bourgeoys whose portrait is on the other wall of the chapel. This step back allows the artist to incorporate into the scene elements missing from the etching: a flag, two figures and a view of the Saint Lawrence River and Mount Royal. The pavilion, strewn with the golden fleurs de lis of the French kingdom, plays a symbolic role, but also acts as a foil by creating depth and isolating the founder in the foreground; his expression is one of serenity; the way he holds his head, his straight back and his gloved left hand holding the other glove show his determination. His strength of character is reinforced by contrasting it with the anxiety shown on the faces of the two subjects in the background. In his isolation, the founder reflects before he acts. His gaze is not turned to the shore on which he will soon land for the first time but is turned inward, confident about the mission ahead.

Even if the historical portrait required little creativity of the artist, Leduc succeeded in showing his originality in the portraits he painted for Notre-Dame-de-Bon-Secours Chapel. He was able to do justice to his models and bring out their personality, their social position and especially their moral qualities — qualities that, in this instance, must be bearers of a message and a lesson.

Monique Lanthier, art historian

PAINTING OF MAISONNEUVE BY OZIAS LEDUC

Photograph: Rachel Gaudreau, Marguerite Bourgeoys Museum

OZIAS LEDUC used this print of the founder of the chapel as the model for his painting.

Taken from *Histoire de la vie de M. Paul de Chomedey, sieur de Maisonneuve, fondateur et premier gouverneur de Ville-Marie*, Pierre Rousseau, S.S., Librairie Saint-Joseph, 1886.

elimination of the trompe l'oeil paintings may not, then, have been the only reason for the renovations in those years. The interior lighting, converted to electricity within the previous year, was not yet effective enough for a building of that size. The somewhat monochromatic paintings of Meloche, as well as the grisaille of the windows, probably made people feel that a brighter interior was needed. One thing is certain: Beaulieu's decoration, even if it was not irreversible, — did he realize it? — would transform the aesthetic quality of Bon-Secours for decades to come.

At Beaulieu's request, the artist Ozias Leduc painted five works: two small paintings of Maisonneuve and of Marguerite Bourgeoys and a large crowning of the Blessed Virgin on the vault of the sanctuary flanked by two paintings of angels on the side walls. The painting of the crowning of the Blessed Virgin was spoiled by a poor restoration in the 1950s and waits in storage for eventual restoration. Despite this loss, the present-day vault of the sanctuary still exhibits a painting of the crowning of Mary, but it is the work of Meloche. The marble communion rail with its bronze doors separating the sanctuary from the nave is signed *T. Carli Edit Roman Bronze Works Inc., N.Y.* This manufacturer had an office in Old Montreal as well. D.A. Beaulieu was also asked to replace the windows of the nave with brightly coloured glass windows that would portray scenes in the life of the Blessed Virgin. Finally, behind the main altar is the large painting of the Assumption, copied from a painting by Murillo

.

THE LAST FOOTHOLD
OF THE CONGREGATION IN OLD MONTREAL

Like the other religious communities in the old city, the Congrégation de Notre-Dame found itself under increasing pressure to leave the site of its foundation and locate elsewhere. In 1854, the community had acquired the Monklands estate on the western side of Mount Royal. This property had, for a few years, been rented by the crown as a residence for the Governor General. There Lord Elgin had taken refuge during the riots that followed the signing of the Rebellion Losses

Bill in 1849 and the burning of the parliament buildings housed in the *marché* Sainte-Anne in Old Montreal. When those events led to the end of Montreal's brief period as capital of the province of Canada (1844 - 1849), Monklands became a hotel. Now the residence became the Villa Maria, a boarding school for girls. Later in the century, it was decided that there was room on the extensive estate for a new house for the Congrégation de Notre-Dame. An impressive building known as the Mountain Mother House was completed on the grounds in 1880.

The Mountain Mother House was to have a very short history. There, early in the afternoon of 8 June 1893, a fire broke out during repairs to the roof. The firemen, summoned by telephone to "the mother house of the Congregation", made the mistake of going first to what was now the former mother house on *rue* Saint-Jean-Baptiste in Old Montreal where the Congregation still conducted a boarding school. That delay, coupled with the difficulty of getting water up the mountain, proved fatal. The new building was totally destroyed. In the aftermath of the fire, the Congregation returned to their old mother house on *rue* Saint-Jean-Baptiste, "to drink of the spirit of the Congregation at its very spring", wrote the Superior General of the time. But the return was only temporary; the old Congregation property lay in the way of the extension of *rue* (now *boulevard*) Saint-Laurent to the port and its years, if not its days, were numbered. Another new mother house was erected, this time on Sherbrooke Street just west of Atwater (now Dawson College), and the community moved there in 1908.

The building erected by the Sulpicians in 1893 to house Bonsecours School was supplied with everything necessary for "furnishing, decoration, and comfort". The annals of the school state that though, like the schools of the *faubourgs* Saint-Laurent and Saint-Antoine, this was a school intended exclusively for the education of poor children — few went beyond the fourth grade — an attempt was made to provide all the courses necessary to permit those who could to continue their education at a more advanced level. The sisters who

THE BUILDING THAT HOUSED THE NEW SCHOOL, constructed by the Sulpicians in 1893.
Archives of the Congrégation de Notre-Dame, Montreal

MOTHER HOUSE OF THE
CONGRÉGATION DE NOTRE-DAME,
RUE SAINT-JEAN BAPTISTE.
View from the inner courtyard.

Oil on canvas, George Delfosse
(1869 - 1939), n.d.

Photograph: Bernard Dubois,
Marguerite Bourgeoys Museum

taught there lived at the old house on *rue* Saint Jean-Baptiste and travelled back and forth.

The contract ceding to the "conseil de Ville-Marie" the old mother house of the Congrégation de Notre-Dame, all the land it occupied and all its dependencies, including Notre-Dame-de-Pitié chapel erected in 1856, was signed on 3 May 1912. The sum paid was $617,000. On 12 July, the annals of the Congrégation de Notre-Dame at Bonsecours School record, the bursar general of the Congregation and the superior of the former mother house handed over the keys "that the sisters of the C.N.D. had held from the cradle of the colony, that is, for 256 years." At this time, and after much discussion, a last-minute decision was made to establish a residence in Bonsecours

School for the sisters teaching there. The annals of the school describe the scene:

> As there was very little time remaining before the house was transferred to the city, we hurried to move to the new residence all that was meant for it; vehicles were quickly piled with luggage, and, pell-mell, we transported and placed in the room opposite the entry: cots, crucifix, soap, bedsprings, religious pictures and engravings, quilts, butter, flour, mattresses, trestles, chiffoniers, potatoes, etc. ... etc. ... The room was packed, and not the least area ready for anything to be put in place.

By the end of August, however, the living area was ready and Bonsecours School thus became the last residence of the Congrégation de Notre-Dame in Old Montreal.

The annals of Bonsecours School also record some interesting information about the disappearance of the old mother house on *rue* Saint Jean-Baptiste. In April 1913, one of the sisters walked over to the site of the demolition and later recorded a long conversation she had held with the contractor whose company had undertaken the work. He remarked on the "magnificent construction ... built to endure several centuries". When she asked if he had discovered any antiquities, his reply suggests that such historical sites did not then receive the care they do today:

> No, sister, not exactly. We did find something in the foundations: the portrait of Mother Bourgeoys, documents recording the time of the construction, rosaries and bits of rosaries, medals. A worker found a medal of Our Lady of the Rosary carrying the date, clearly visible, of 1692; he refused $7.00 for it, there are always ladies and young girls coming to buy these souvenirs. We also found two axes, hammers and a sabre. We also discovered two trenches; a deep one leading to the river and a shallower one going toward Notre-Dame-de-Pitié Church.

THE 1950S AT THE CHAPEL: CELEBRATION AND TRANSFORMATION

After the major transformation at the end of the nineteenth and beginning of the twentieth centuries, the chapel remained largely unchanged for several decades. In a 1941 interview with *Le Devoir* newspaper, M. Henri Legrand, S.S., the longest serving chaplain in the history of Notre-Dame-de-Bon-Secours (1918 - 1942), affirmed that there had been no changes to the chapel in twenty-five years. Although restoration work was done in the chapel by Alphonse Lespérance in the second half of the 1940s, there were no major alterations in the appearance of the chapel until the 1950s. But that prosperous post-war decade saw many physical changes in both the interior and the exterior of the chapel. Some of the changes were prompted by the beatification of the chapel's founder, Marguerite Bourgeoys, some by a need for repairs, and others by the observance of the three-hundredth anniversary of the founding of the chapel and the hundredth anniversary of the restoration of pilgrimage by Bishop Bourget. For better or worse, this period gave the interior of the chapel much of its present appearance although the restorations of the 1990s would obliterate many twentieth-century changes in favour of earlier decorative elements, of which the most striking are the works of Meloche.

Marguerite Bourgeoys was beatified by Pope Pius XII on 12 November 1950. This last formal step before canonization naturally awakened new interest in her life: it also gave rise to a number of ceremonies of public veneration. On 30 April 1951, the very first Marguerite Bourgeoys Museum was inaugurated in a room beneath the sanctuary of the chapel. There, in sixty-seven small glass cases, miniatures were used to portray the life of Marguerite Bourgeoys. These were the work of Sister Hélène Perrault, with the help of a group composed of sisters of the Congregation and members and friends of the Perrault family. Several artists and artisans collaborated: the heads of the male figures in the various groupings, for instance, were carved by Joseph Guardo, the Montreal sculptor, and some of the tiny chairs, by Julien Bourgault of Saint-Jean-Port-Joli. Some of the small figures came from as far away as Italy and Troyes in France. The miniatures were restored in 1962 thanks to the generous financial and technical assistance of David M. Stewart. The museum also contained the banner depicting Marguerite Bourgeoys which had hung at Saint Peter's Basilica in Rome during the beatification ceremony in

Henri Legrand, S.S., Chaplain at Notre-Dame-de-Bon-Secours

Monsieur Legrand was born in Paris in 1875. He became a Sulpician and came to Montreal in 1900 where, for four years he taught, first at the Collège de Montréal and then at the Grand Séminaire. Wishing to exercise a pastoral ministry, he became curate at Notre-Dame and devoted himself especially to the schools of the area including Bonsecours School. The annals of that school for Friday, 11 September 1914 record: "Our good Father Legrand is going to leave us … His mother country in danger calls out to him strongly and our hearts are wrung to see him on his farewell visit today." The annals also contain a black-edged letter from Marseille dated 18 November 1916. In it, M. Legrand thanks the sisters of Bonsecours school for their expressions of condolence on the death of his brother in the war. He ends, "My situation remains the same. I am still attached to the same hospital train of the first stage of the *Armée d'Orient*." (He served as a priest-nurse). In December 1916, however, came the joyful news of his return to Montreal as chaplain of Notre-Dame-de-Bon-Secours as well as curate of Notre-Dame.

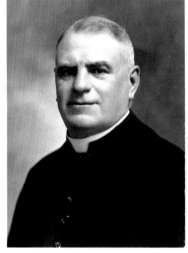

M. Henri Legrand, S.S.
Archives of the Congrégation de
Notre-Dame de Montréal

During his years as chaplain, M. Legrand welcomed as many as seventy or seventy-five pilgrimages to the chapel during the month of May. He was able to prevail upon the Congrégation de Notre-Dame to return to the chapel the statuette of Notre-Dame-de-Bon-Secours missing since 1831, an event which took place 10 April 1935. M. Legrand was to remain chaplain for nearly three decades, taking a lively interest in the children who attended the school and in their families, wise and gentle in the confessional, compassionate toward the sick. Over the years, the annals bear frequent witness to the kindness that made him much beloved in the Bonsecours area. He was a familiar figure in Bonsecours Market where he was often given a cucumber, a vegetable of which he was very fond, on his way home to the seminary in the evening.

On 8 January 1942, M. Legrand left Notre-Dame-de-Bon-Secours Chapel at 5:10 p.m. to go to his confessional in Notre-Dame Church. At 6 p.m. the sisters were shocked to learn of the sudden death in that confessional of one they did not hesitate to call "the soul of Bonsecours School".

MINIATURES FROM THE FIRST MARGUERITE BOURGEOYS MUSEUM created in 1951 tell the story of the life of the founder, each scene in a separate display case. These miniatures are an integral part of the present museum.

Photograph: Rachel Gaudreau, Marguerite Bourgeoys Museum

THE FIRST MARGUERITE BOURGEOYS MUSEUM located in a room under the sanctuary of Notre-Dame-de-Bon-Secours Chapel.

Photograph: Rachel Gaudreau, Marguerite Bourgeoys Museum

1950 and an altar from Notre-Dame-des-Neiges Cemetery.

From 1953 to 1957 the administrator of the chapel was M. Lambert Desaulniers, S.S., who undertook an extensive programme of repairs and renovations. Among the most visible were the alterations made to the tower and the steeple, deemed necessary because of structural weaknesses and depradations caused by weather conditions over the years. The immense statue of the Virgin overlooking the port was lowered more than seven metres by the removal of the base on which it was lodged. The angels, too, were lowered because the columns on which they stood had been rotted by rain. The steeple in front of the chapel lost part of its double lantern and took on the simpler form of an earlier era. Both the steeple and the dome above the observation deck in the tower were covered in copper like the rest of the roof. These changes gave both the tower and the steeple their present appearance.

In preparation for the three-hundredth anniversary of the founding of the chapel celebrated in 1957, M. Desaulniers entrusted the interior decoration of the chapel to an Italian artist, Giocondo Vorano. Vorano designed four mosaics that were executed in Venice. The first of these was unveiled by Paul-Émile Cardinal Léger on 1

FAÇADE OF THE CHAPEL initially designed by the architects Perrault and Mesnard and modified in the middle of the twentieth century.

Photograph: Rachel Gaudreau, Marguerite Bourgeoys Museum

THE TOWER WAS ALSO CHANGED to lighten the weight of the heavy structure behind the chapel. Several angels and the three theological virtues created by the sculptor Laperle were removed from their pedestals.

Photograph: Rachel Gaudreau, Marguerite Bourgeoys Museum

December 1957. Hung on the sanctuary wall to the right of the main altar, it depicted Bishop Bourget's presentation of the *Vierge dorée* in 1848 while Cardinal Léger, as donor of the mosaic in 1957, appears on his knees in the right foreground. A matching mosaic on the wall to the left of the altar, also his gift, was unveiled by Cardinal Léger on 30 April 1958. This depicted the first attempt to found the chapel in 1657. On 30 November 1958, small mosaics of Bishop Bourget and of the Baron de Fancamp were unveiled near the two side altars. In 1959, a life-size statue of Marguerite Bourgeoys carved in linden wood by Joseph Guardo was placed in the chapel.

Further renovations of the chapel were entrusted to the architect Eugène Perron in 1958. Modifications were made to provide a wider central aisle and two side aisles. The wooden floor was replaced with rubber tiles and the side walls were lined with ceramic tile. Oak benches with leatherette kneelers were installed and inner doors and confessionals replaced. The Sisters of the Holy Cross who were then modernizing their mother house in Ville Saint-Laurent presented the chapel with twelve chandeliers from their old chapel.

THE SPIRITUAL ROLE OF THE CHAPEL

The records of Notre-Dame-de-Bon-Secours Chapel make it clear that Bishop Bourget had been successful in his effort to re-establish the chapel as a place of pilgrimage. Each year the chapel drew pilgrims not just from the local area but from many other parts of Canada and the United States. Certain groups maintained a long tradition of yearly pilgrimage to the chapel: the Apostolate of the Sea, the Snowshoers, and the Papal Zouaves who still arrive at the chapel in full panoply each September. English as well as French schools and parishes continued their yearly visits to the chapel, including Saint Patrick's Parish that maintained the tradition of returning to its "cradle" even after the Sulpicians had been replaced by secular priests as pastors. The months of October and, above all, of May, the two months dedicated to the Blessed Virgin Mary, were the high points of ceremonies at the chapel. Usually several groups of pilgrims arrived

each day: on 24 May 1957, for example, six masses were celebrated, the first at 6:30 a.m., the last at 9 p.m. and there were also two hours of prayer organized.

Since the days of Bishop Bourget, it had been the custom for the bishop of Montreal to come to the chapel on 30 April to initiate the devotions marking the month of Mary. In the 1950s, Paul-Émile Léger, Montreal's first cardinal-archbishop, emulated his predecessor in making of this a popular and picturesque event. On 30 April 1953, the population of Montreal was invited to a ceremony that began at 8 p.m. in Notre-Dame Church. There the cardinal preached to a

TWO OF FOUR MOSAICS DONATED BY PAUL-ÉMILE CARDINAL LÉGER in 1957 to celebrate the three hundredth anniversary of the founding of the chapel. They are the work of the Italian artist, G.Vorano.

Archives of the Marguerite Bourgeoys Museum

Dock workers' pilgrimage in the chapel in 1958. Like the sailors before them, the dock workers developed a special connection with the chapel. Their daughters attended Bonsecours School and belonged to the choir that sang at Mass. Every year, on the occasion of their pilgrimage, the dock workers made an offering that allowed their daughters and the teachers to enjoy a school outing.

Archives of the
Marguerite Bourgeoys Museum

packed church while those who could not find places listened to his sermon over loudspeakers in Place d'Armes. After benediction of the Blessed Sacrament, a torchlight procession, singing and praying, accompanied the cardinal along *rue* Notre-Dame and down *rue* Bonsecours to a special dais set up behind Notre-Dame-de-Bon-Secours Chapel on *rue* de la Commune. Cardinal Léger carried the statuette of Notre-Dame-de-Bon-Secours. The edition of *La Presse* for 1 May 1953 contains the following description:

> At a certain moment, *rue* Notre-Dame, from *rue* Bon-Secours to Place d'Armes, was nothing but a large carpet of heads and flames beneath which roads and sidewalks disappeared. The exterior of the historic chapel of Notre-Dame-de-Bon-Secours was completely illuminated last evening, and the large statue that towers over the dome, radiant with light, seemed to open protective arms over the crowd of 15,000 faithful gathered below.

OPENING CEREMONIES OF THE MONTH OF MAY 1953 over which Paul-Émile Cardinal Léger presided before an attendance of 15,000 people.

La Presse, 1 May 1953

The little girls of Bonsecours School, dressed in white, had strewn flowers before the statuette; now they stood in a place of honour near the dais and heard the cardinal consecrate the archdiocese of Montreal to the Blessed Virgin Mary.

Gertrude Beaupré-Trottier

Just when it seemed that not a single family would remain in Old Montreal, one family made the decision to live in the Bonsecours area and to establish their business there. In 1963, at a time when the house of Jacques Viger had just been demolished, Gertrude Beaupré-Trottier, with her husband Jean-Jacques Trottier and their seven children, ranging in age from seven to twenty-two years, moved into premises near the corner of Bonsecours and Saint-Paul streets. The family restored the building and established what was to become a flourishing restaurant.

MADAME GERTRUDE TROTTIER
Photograph: M.F. Aaron

For Madame Trottier it was important that Ville-Marie had, from its origins, been consecrated to the Holy Family of Nazareth. She was conscious of the great women who had been the first to support families in Montreal through the establishment of a hospital, a school and an institution offering services to the unfortunate. She was also conscious of other women, less famous but just as important, who were the mothers of the earliest families. In honour of those courageous women, she named her restaurant Les Filles du Roy and she chose to locate it in the shadow of the little chapel rather than in a more obviously commercial locale.

Madame Trottier, a nurse by profession, had been among the pioneers of Notre-Dame Hospital before devoting herself to the care of her growing family. But her attention was not limited to her own family: she always took an interest in the larger society. During her years in Old Montreal, she was involved in the arts and in historical and genealogical societies where she worked for the preservation of the Quebec heritage. She participated actively in the charitable organizations of the Bonsecours area, the Accueil Bonneau and the Porte du Ciel, and offered help to neighbours in need. She died on 10 March 1997.

GOODBYE TO THE LITTLE SCHOOL

The decline of Montreal as the metropolis of Canada and the rise of Toronto, which had an immediate impact on the lives and the living space of ordinary people, was to some extent tied to one historical event that affected more than just the history of Montreal. The opening of the Saint Lawrence Seaway in 1959 made it possible for ocean-going ships to continue their way up the Saint Lawrence to Toronto and the Great Lakes; thus, Montreal lost its status as the final sea port in the interior of the continent. This shift of economic forces dealt a

THE PUPILS OF BONSECOURS SCHOOL attend a religious ceremony in the chapel in 1958.

National Film Board of Canada, no. 64580

severe blow to the city. The old town lost its attractiveness in the eyes of commerce and the business centre of Montreal shifted to the west. The result was yet another uprooting and exodus from Old Montreal which, this time, saw the departure of most of the larger institutions and enterprises except for some legal and administrative institutions that remained in the historic centre. In the 1960s, Old Montreal took on the depressing air of a forgotten district, down on its luck.

The 1960s were also discouraging years at Bonsecours School, attached to the Montreal Catholic School Commission since June 1930. The population of the Bonsecours district was in decline and the trend in education was away from small neighbourhood schools in favour of sending children to larger schools which would serve a wider area. The annals of Bonsecours School contain an ominous entry for September 1961:

> The pupils are back. Eighty-three are registered. Each year the number of pupils goes down. The city is planning great projects of urbanization in our area that will result in the disappearance not only of the slums but of all the houses without character to leave only buildings of historic interest. Bonsecours Market itself, it is said, is in its final year. This explains why families are looking for homes elsewhere, so as not to find themselves without lodging if they are suddenly ordered to move.

On 3 September 1963, only sixty pupils were registered, forty-four girls and sixteen boys in five grades; on 6 September, the school commission ordered the transfer of the fourteen pupils in grades four and five to Notre-Dame School which also lacked pupils. Though a kindergarten class with fifteen children was opened at the school in March 1965, the elementary school continued to decline: in 1967-68 there were just thirty-three children in four grades (grouped in two classes). On 11 April 1968, the blow fell: the school commission announced that the school would close at the end of the school year. It had been in existence for 130 years and during most of that time had served the children of the Bonsecours area, boys as well as girls.

The journal kept by the chaplain, M. Jean Langis, S.S., during those years reflects the same decline in the population of the area.

Though the chapel was not a parish, the chaplain regularly visited the Catholic residents of the area and each year entered the results of the census he had compiled. In May 1963, the number of Catholics in the district was 1225; there were 151 families. By February 1968, the numbers had fallen to 700 persons, 77 families, a decline of almost half the population over a space of five years. The number of persons living on their own or in religious institutions declined in the same period from 650 in 1963 to 325 in 1968.

Obviously, it is easy to guess that the city did not undertake the renewal of Old Montreal anticipated by the Bonsecours annalist. Apart from one or two office towers and several large parking lots that resulted from this period, the old city was largely spared the great building projects that would have changed the historical character of the area forever. Nevertheless, the district was to emerge from its lean years slowly, very slowly. Side by side with the spectacular happening that was Expo 67 and that propelled Quebec once and for all into the modern age, Old Montreal began to re-assert its own identity. Private initiatives and government protection had an impact; Old Montreal was classified as a historic district in 1964. The residents of the *faubourg* Bonsecours and of Old Montreal may have abandoned the area, but a significant event would call them back: in 1992, Montreal celebrated its 350th birthday. Many institutions would begin to adopt a new image, others would be built. And the chapel had not spoken its last word ...

A RETURN
TO THE ORIGINS

Battered by the years, at times transformed and embellished, at times neglected, the chapel seems to have rediscovered the fulness of its identity in the closing years of the twentieth century. With this rediscovery came the desire to make known to new generations its considerable historical significance in Old Montreal. The last decade of the millennium was rich with unexpected developments for Notre-Dame-de-Bon-Secours. In a very short time and as the result of happy coincidence or the unforeseen combination of circumstances, the different layers of the history of the chapel — and of its prehistory — began to emerge like so many forgotten facets of a precious stone that suddenly sparkle in the sunlight. The founding institutions agreed to establish the Notre-Dame-de-Bon-Secours Chapel/Marguerite Bourgeoys Museum in its present form. So the dream became a reality with contributions from archaeology, art and architectural history, architects' plans and the design work of restoration specialists.

THE CHAPEL: SOME CANVAS COMES UNDONE...

In 1994, the Sulpicians decided to replace the roofing of the chapel and to improve the insulation under the roof. The change in humidity that resulted from the alterations caused a section of the decorative canvas installed in 1908 by Delphis Adolphe Beaulieu to come loose. When that section of the vault was inspected, it was discovered that Beaulieu had not destroyed the paintings by Meloche but had simply glued his own canvases over them. For almost a century, Beaulieu's decorative canvas had served as a protective covering for Meloche's works. This discovery provoked renewed interest in the chapel.

A CORNER OF THE CANVAS PAINTED by D.A. Beaulieu comes loose in 1994 uncovering one of Meloche's murals.

Photograph: Robin Simard, Marguerite Bourgeoys Museum

RESTORATION OF THE VAULT of the chapel. After D.A. Beaulieu's decorative canvases were removed from the vault of the chapel, they were stored in the basement of the Cathedral of Marie Reine-du-Monde.

Photograph: Robin Simard, Marguerite Bourgeoys Museum

MOVING THE FURNISHINGS of the sanctuary during the 1997 work.

Photograph: Alain Laforest

Thanks to the financial contributions of the ministère de la Culture et des Communications du Québec and the Priests of Saint Sulpice, Meloche's fine murals once more saw the light of day. Beaulieu's canvas was removed — rolled up and carefully stored — and Meloche's works restored. The glue covering the paintings was removed with hot water and some of the paintings were touched up. Still, no one would have guessed that this was but the beginning of an amazing adventure that would result in the discovery of the deepest elements of the chapel's past.

THE MUSEUM: THE FOUNDATIONS ARE UNCOVERED
At about the same time, the Congrégation de Notre-Dame decided to move the Marguerite Bourgeoys Centre that, until then, had always been located at the mother house. Opened in 1952, the purpose of the Centre was to make known the life and work of Marguerite Bourgeoys. In 1985, the mother house itself was moved from its location at the corner of Sherbrooke and Atwater to the former *collège* Marguerite Bourgeoys on Westmount Avenue. In 1995, after serious

RESTORATION OF THE VAULT IN PROGRESS.

Photograph: Robin Simard, Marguerite Bourgeoys Museum

The painting of
the Presentation of Mary
after restoration.

Photograph: Alain Laforest

consideration, the sisters decided to move the Centre closer to the historical and geographical foundations of the Congregation and to the Old Montreal neighbourhood where Marguerite Bourgeoys — since 1982 Saint Marguerite Bourgeoys — had spent her life. This new location had the added advantage of easy public access. The choice was to house the Centre in the old Bonsecours School. Since the school was closed in 1968, it had served as residence for the sisters who cared for the chapel, sacristy and the small Marguerite Bourgeoys Museum and worked on various other educational projects.

The idea of renovating this museum dedicated to the founder had begun to develop into a concrete plan. The Marguerite Bourgeoys Centre already had a small collection of objects relating to Marguerite Bourgeoys and the history of the Congregation, including the Pierre Le Ber portrait of Marguerite. The plan was to continue to exhibit this collection in a modest museum that would also include the min-

iatures depicting the life of Marguerite Bourgeoys already on view on the site in Old Montreal. But the ancient site of the chapel seemed to have plans of its own.

The renovation of the school began at the end of 1996. The chosen architect, Maurice Desnoyers, drew up plans that suggested using the old classroom space for the museum areas, retaining the size of the five rooms, the old woodwork, the wooden floors and the hallways to recall the original purpose of the building. In the basement, however, the plans called for major changes in order to provide storage space and rooms that would serve as a residence. That was the

THE EXTERIOR WALL OF THE CHAPEL covered with cement since the end of the nineteenth century.

Photograph: Rachel Gaudreau, Marguerite Bourgeoys Museum

THE 1997-1998 RENOVATIONS were an opportunity to uncover the original stone work and to remove the opaque exterior double glazing replacing it with transparent tempered glass.

Photograph: Rachel Gaudreau, Marguerite Bourgeoys Museum

moment when the archaeologists of the Groupe de recherches en histoire du Québec arrived on the scene and the project began to assume proportions never anticipated at the outset. The architect summed up the main discoveries to which the reorganization project gave rise:

No one foresaw then that the stone wall at the north end (of the 1784 attached building) would be identified as the archaeological remains of the foundation walls of buildings contemporary with the 1771 chapel... The original plans that involved tearing them down were revised and this gift offered by the site was incorporated into the general planning. The excavations turned up important artefacts catalogued by the ministère de la Culture et des Communications du Québec...

The dynamic return of Saint Marguerite Bourgeoys to Old Montreal where her mission to New France had begun proved to be the trigger that set in motion extraordinary discoveries. The relocation of the Marguerite Bourgeoys Centre from Westmount to the rooms of the old neighbourhood school and the adjoining buildings soon became more than a simple move. The discovery of the foundations of the old central building brought back the whole story connected with the warehouse called *La Friponne* and its shady activities. The sensational recovery of the entire work of Meloche on the vault of the chapel, the archaeological richness of the stone work of the half-dome vault of the crypt, the restoration of the angels with trumpets by the experts of the Centre de conservation du Québec and finally the absolutely extraordinary and unexpected archaeological finds in the cellar of the present chapel were incorporated into the initial plans for the museum to make of it a public institution that is one of a kind.[1]

In fact, once the foundations of the attached building were protected and the vault of the crypt stripped, the archaeological discoveries continued. Excitement knew no bounds when the archaeologists responsible for the field work revealed two major discoveries. The researchers had found remains of Amerindian prehistory and, above all, they had uncovered the ruins of the first stone chapel founded by Marguerite Bourgeoys and destroyed by fire in 1754. Suddenly, the purpose of this space intended as a storage area had to be reconsidered. The discoveries made here were of major significance to the

THE CELLAR THAT SERVED AS STORAGE AREA before the archaeological dig.

Photograph: Pierre Fauteux, Ville de Montréal

THE ARCHAEOLOGICAL SITE ONCE THE DIG AND RESTORATIONS WERE COMPLETED. Shown are the remains of the first stone chapel founded by Marguerite Bourgeoys (1675-1678).

Photograph: Rachel Gaudreau, Marguerite Bourgeoys Museum

1. Maurice DESNOYERS, *Chapelle Notre-Dame-de-Bon-Secours, Musée Marguerite Bourgeoys et le patrimoine architectural*, Montreal, Musée Marguerite-Bourgeoys, 1999, pp.23-25. Trans.

THE "DISCOVERY ROOM" where artefacts found during the dig are arranged at the foot of the old wall of the attached building of 1784. The Marguerite Bourgeoys Museum was designed and realized by Design+Communication; the texts used in the exhibition are the work of Catalyse communication.

Photograph: Alain Laforest

THE CRYPT, THE VAULTED ROOM where formerly the small Marguerite Bourgeoys Museum was located. Now, objects connected to the history of the chapel are displayed there, along with a scale model of the archaeological site. In the foreground, the statue of Saint Michael the Archangel designed by Gratton et Laperle (1890).

Photograph: Christian Guay, Marguerite Bourgeoys Museum

history of Montreal. This other "gift" offered by the site led the architect to revise his plans and, with the archaeologists, to propose to the Congrégation de Notre-Dame and to the Sulpicians that the site be developed. The archaeological site, a unique place for discovering historical origins, would from then on be part of the new plans for the museum.

The re-opening of Notre-Dame-de-Bon-Secours Chapel and the Marguerite Bourgeoys Museum in 1998 gave Old Montreal a new heritage site. The Sulpicians and the Congrégation de Notre-Dame have together formed a corporation for the management of the site, a logical step for these two religious communities that have been associated with the chapel since its beginnings. Rarely has Montreal been able to offer this kind of continued tradition on a single site. Although it is impossible to know what the future holds for this institution, it is hoped that the circumstances that until now have saved it from

outrageous proposals or changes of purpose will persist for generations to come. In a society where the word "perpetuity" has no real
meaning in practice, who knows what weight will be given to Marguerite Bourgeoys' wish of three centuries ago for Notre-Dame-de-
Bon-Secours? On the threshold of a new millennium, the little chapel
on *rue* Saint-Paul continues to bear witness to Montreal's history
across the centuries and to invite within its walls all who wish to
share its beauty and its peace.

NOTRE-DAME-DE-BON-SECOURS
CHAPEL as seen today.

Photograph: Francesco Bellomo ©

ANGEL WITH TRUMPET

Photograph: Rachel Gaudreau,
Marguerite Bourgeoys Museum

TO LEARN MORE ABOUT NOTRE-DAME-DE-BON-SECOURS CHAPEL AND...

ITS HISTORY, ITS ARCHITECTURE

DESNOYERS, Maurice. *Chapelle Notre-Dame-de-Bon-Secours, Musée Marguerite-Bourgeoys et le patrimoine architectural.* Montreal: Marguerite Bourgeoys Museum 1999.

LAFRAMBOISE, Yves. *La chapelle Bonsecours, Évolution physique du bâtiment et bilan des interventions architecturales.* Ethnotech inc. Unpublished report, 1990.

LEGRIS, Patrick. *Rapport de traitement de conservation de la chapelle Notre-Dame-de-Bon-Secours.* Unpublished report, 1998.

LELEU, Jean-Marie. *Histoire de Notre-Dame de Bon-Secours à Montréal.* Montreal: Cadieux & Derome 1900.

MARTIN, Félix, S.J. *Le Manuel du Pèlerin.* Montreal: Lovell et Gibson 1848.

MARGUERITE BOURGEOYS

SIMPSON, Patricia. *Marguerite Bourgeoys and Montreal, 1640-1665.* Montreal: McGill-Queen's University Press 1997.

THE ARCHAEOLOGICAL DISCOVERIES

Groupe de recherches en histoire du Québec, [François Véronneau, Pierre Jacques Ratio & Claude Joyal], "Inventaire et fouilles archéologiques. Site BjFj-56. Chapelle Notre-Dame-de-Bon-Secours – Musée Marguerite-Bourgeoys", Montreal, unpublished report presented to the Congrégation de Notre-Dame (Marguerite Bourgeoys Museum) and to the ministère de la Culture et des Communications du Québec, 1998.

THE HISTORY OF MONTREAL

ROBERT, Jean-Claude. *Atlas historique de Montréal.* Montreal: Art Global Libre Expression 1994.

ARCHIVAL SOURCES

Archives de la Paroisse Notre-Dame de Montréal
Archives nationales du Québec
Archives du Séminaire de Saint-Sulpice de Montréal
National Archives of Canada